GURKHA

THE ILLUSTRATED HISTORY OF
AN ELITE FIGHTING FORCE

GURKHA
THE ILLUSTRATED HISTORY OF AN ELITE FIGHTING FORCE

CHRISTOPHER CHANT

BLANDFORD PRESS
POOLE · DORSET

First published in the UK 1985 by Blandford
Press, Link House, West Street, Poole, Dorset, BHI5 ILL

Copyright © 1985 Blandford Press Ltd

Distributed in the United States by
Sterling Publishing Co., Inc.,
2 Park Avenue, New York, NY 10016

British Library Cataloguing in Publication Data

Chant, Christopher
 Gurkha: an illustrated history.
 1. Gurkha soldiers—History
 I. Title
 355.3′1   UA853.N35

ISBN 0 7137 1384 4

Typeset in Monophoto Ehrhardt by
August Filmsetting, Haydock, St. Helens.

Printed in Great Britain by
R. J. Acford Ltd., Chichester, Sussex.

*Opposite. An emotive as well as strategic success was the
Fourteenth Army's capture of Mandalay, whose loss by the
Japanese opened the way to central and southern Burma
for the rampaging units of the Fourteenth Army, with
Gurkhas well to the fore of the combat units.*

CONTENTS

The Gurkha orderlies of Field-Marshal The Lord Roberts were nicknamed Shrapnel and Bullethead, and were men of the 5th Gurkhas.

THE
GURKHA

The Gurkhas enjoy a position unique in the modern world, being highly capable soldiers who serve in large numbers under the flags of countries not their own, but who nevertheless enjoy a reputation second to none (with an inordinate number of mythical attributes) and untouched by any of the pejorative connotations of the word 'mercenary'. Though the Gurkhas now serve with other armed forces, the extraordinary fact remains that Gurkha soldiers have served as part of British arms for just under one and three-quarter centuries, winning the total admiration and dedication of their officers and peers, the fear and respect of their enemies, and a highly favoured position in the esteem of the British public, who have come to regard the Gurkhas in a particularly favoured light.

And yet there is, in the purest sense of the word, no such thing as a Gurkha in the ethnic sense. The word is in fact a corruption of Goorkha, a small town and one time state in the north-west of what is now the kingdom of Nepal, a long but comparatively narrow country nestled on the southern side of the Himalayas between two giants, India and China (represented by its satellite Tibet). With an area of some 5500 square miles, and measuring some 520 miles along its east–west axis and an average of 90–100 miles on the north–south axis, Nepal is divided into four main zones, each of them running east–west along the basic line of the Himalayas: bordering northern India is a belt of grassland and jungle (the Terai) varying in depth from 10 to 30 miles; behind this is the Dhun, a line of low sandstone hills; north again from this is the hill country formed by the foothills of the Himalayas, rising to an altitude of some 10,000 ft (3048 m.); and in the north of the country are the Himalayas proper above the 10,000-ft altitude. The religious and ethnic background of modern Nepal is extremely mixed: the Rajputs and Aryans who arrived in the area during the fighting against the Mongols brought with them Hinduism, while the rest of the country, represented by the Magar, Gurung, Limbu and Rai tribes of Mongolian origins, are generally of

A task not infrequently entrusted to the Gurkhas for their speed and good musketry was that of forming the rearguard, as in this illustration of the 4th Gurkhas in 1911 somewhere on the North-West Frontier.

Subadar Major Gurung Gurkha of the 2nd King Edward's Own Gurkha Rifles (The Sirmoor Rifles) was the last Indian Orderly Officer of King Edward VII.

the Buddhist persuasion. The racial mixture and geography of Nepal have produced a people of relatively small but robust constitution, notable for the extreme cheerfulness of their disposition and the endurance of their constitutions.

During a long and extremely varied history, Nepal has expanded and contracted with its varying fortunes, but may be regarded as generally fragmentary in the first half of the 18th century, which was the period in which European matters began to affect the region to any great extent. The background to the period is the decline of the Moghul empire as a result of internal problems and external pressures from an expanding European influence. Nevertheless, during the 18th century the Moghuls had secured the nominal allegiance of various small states in the northern Indian plain between the Sutlej and Teesta rivers in return for a nominal Moghul assurance of protection against the raids launched on an almost traditional basis by the various hill tribes to the north.

Matters might have continued for some time in their traditional order had not Prithi Narayan Sah, the ruler of the Goorkha hill state, been astute enough to realize that events in Bengal were heralding a new era for the Indian sub-continent. For in Bengal the British were making considerable gains in the military and economic fields as a result of the considerably superior organization of their army. Prithi Narayan Sah realized that by adopting the European standard of uniformity and discipline in his troops, he could secure a decisive qualitative edge over his neighbours. Thus Goorkha raised a relatively small but well disciplined body of troops more than a match for the state's opponents. Initial moves were made against a number of small chiefdoms, fully vindicating the efficiency of the new system, and the Goorkhas were soon faced with a more formidable opponent in Mir Cosim Ali, the Nabob of Moorshedabad, who took it upon himself to contain the menace now posed by Goorkha. But in 1762 the nabob was soundly defeated, and by 1768 Prithi Narayan Sah had been declared king of Nepal, with his capital in Katmandu. Not even the arrival of an ill-organized expedition mounted by the government of Bengal in 1766 could prevent the overthrow of the Rajah of Nepal. Prithi Narayan Sah died in 1775, having conquered most of the present-day kingdom of Nepal.

Prithi Narayan Sah was followed by equally able successors, and in the next 30 years the kingdom of Nepal became a state to be feared: to the east the Nepalese occupied Sikkim and invaded Tibet, to the annoyance of the Chinese, who launched a large offensive to eliminate the Nepalese. This campaign came within an ace of capturing Katmandu, but a peace settlement restored the status quo with the Nepalese still in control of Sikkim. However, it was clear that further expansion in this direction would incur the renewed hostility of China, so Nepalese attention was diverted to the west, where successes were achieved in Kumaon, Garhwal, the Dun valley and the Dogra hills on the approaches to Kashmir. But again the Nepalese came up against formidable opponents, this time the Sikhs led by the Maharajah Ranjit Singh, who checked Nepal's westward urge in the Kangra valley. What had emerged from these various campaigns was the military superiority of the

An official issue kukri of World War I vintage shows off the salient features of this first-class weapon, whose weight and shape make it a superior close-quarter weapon to the bayonet, sword and pike. A considerable mythology has sprung up around the kukri, most of it patently untrue. The notch above the hilt allows a Gurkha to catch his opponent's blade and, with a twist, disarm him before the killing stroke is delivered. The scabbard of the issue kukri has a pocket sized to accept a purse and two small knives, one sharp for general use and the other dull for use as a hone.

Gurkhas in terms of basic capability and organization, but also the problems associated with relatively limited manpower (as was inevitable in a mountain kingdom) when faced by opponents from the plain regions with considerably larger manpower reserves. Nevertheless, the tactical superiority of the Gurkhas was readily apparent (the more so since the defeat of the ill-advised expedition of 1766 mounted by the British). With its basic strength, the Nepalese kingdom was an ideal base for continued small-scale operations into plain regions.

Throughout this period the Honourable East India Company had been trying to reach an accommodation with the Gurkhas, who were beginning to make inroads into areas under British tutelage, but the arrogance of the Gurkhas made this impossible. The kingdom steadfastly refused to entertain the allocation of a British Resident in Katmandu, and the British had to tread warily lest they antagonize what was by local standards a formidable enemy.

By the beginning of the 18th century, therefore, the kingdom of Nepal was beginning to be a considerable thorn in the side of the Honourable East India Company, with a decisive moment approaching as the spheres of influence dominated by each side came ever closer as the aggressive Gurkhas took every opportunity to bring smaller states under their domination. This conflicted most seriously with the interests of the local Indian rulers: in the British sphere of influence, rulers were left in control of their domains on payment of an annual tribute to the Honourable East India Company; but under the Gurkha regime the previous rulers and their families were executed, their places being taken by Gurkhas. For this reason local feeling, at least amongst the ruling classes, was inclined towards the British rather than the Gurkhas.

The depot at Dehra Dun has several memorials to the deeds of Gurkhas who had been based there, the two best known being those at the base of Kalunga Hill.

'An Assemblage of Ghoorkas', an aquatint after an illustration by J.B. Trazer, was published in 1820 as one of a series, 'Views on the Himalaya Mountains'. Shields were common with the Gurkhas of the period, surviving as late as 1858 when they featured amongst the equipment of the newly-raised Hazara Goorkha Battalion (25th Punjab Infantry).

THIS IS INSCRIBED
AS A TRIBUTE OF RESPECT
FOR OUR GALLANT ADVERSARY
BULBUDDER
COMMANDER OF THE FORT
AND HIS BRAVE GOORKAS
WHO WERE AFTERWARDS
WHILE IN THE SERVICE
OF RUNJEET SING
SHOT DOWN IN THEIR RANKS
TO THE LAST MAN
BY AFGHAN ARTILLERY.

The wording on one of the monuments at Kalunga Hill can only hint at the courage and savagery of the Afghan wars.

The dominant force in Nepal from 1846 to 1877, when he died, was the Maharajah Sir Jung Bahadur Kunwar Rana, who supported the British fully during the disastrous days of the Indian Mutiny in 1857.

ON THE HIGHEST POINT
OF THE HILL ABOVE THIS TOMB
STOOD THE FORT OF KALUNGR
AFTER TWO ASSAULTS
ON THE 31ST OCT AND 27TH NOVER
IT WAS CAPTD BY THE BRITISH TROOPS
ON THE 30TH OF NOVEMBER
AND COMPLETELY RAZD TO THE GROUND

A classic moment in military history as the wounded Piper Findlater of The Gordon Highlanders pipes his comrades into action in support of the Gurkhas pinned down in the Battle of Dargai Heights on 20 October 1897 during the Tirah campaign.

Kalunga itself was a decisive moment in the history of Nepal, and though the Gurkha defence was overcome by the British in 1814, it was only after the British had received more than ample demonstration of the Gurkhas' martial will and capability.

A Gurkha sepoy, circa *1816*

THE NEPAL WAR
& EARLY BRITISH
SERVICE

The state that finally triggered a direct confrontation between the British and the Gurkhas was Oudh, which was within the British sphere of influence and protection, but nonetheless coveted by the Gurkhas, whose king was at this time a minor. Thus real power in Nepal was exercised by the Thappa family: two members of this family held the most important positions in the land, Bheem Sein being the prime minister and his brother-in-law Umur Sing commander-in-chief of the army.

In 1813 Gurkha forces swept into Oudh and in addition to a considerable amount of raiding took and garrisoned the region of Bhutwal on the Oudh side of the frontier with Nepal. Yet again Indian appeals to the British were made, and this time it was decided that the Nepalese must finally be taught a lesson. The administration in Bengal demanded an immediate withdrawal by the Gurkhas from all disputed territories, but the Gurkhas flatly refused. Negotiations were initiated by Lord Moira, the new Governor General of Bengal in succession to Lord Minto, but it soon became clear that actions would have to supplant words. The British negotiators were recalled, and a force of troops despatched from Goruchpur to seize the Bhutwal region. The Gurkhas withdrew in the face of this expedition, and Bhutwal was restored to its rightful lords. However, with the situation apparently stable the British forces were withdrawn, and into this vacuum the Gurkhas immediately returned. In Bhutwal itself they stormed three police stations, killing or wounding 24 of the occupants, and killed the local British officer.

Moira felt that he had gone far enough towards meeting the demands of the Gurkhas, and in November 1814 declared war on Nepal. The resulting Nepal War was to mark a decisive turning point in Anglo–Nepalese relations, for in the face of a substantial invasion force the Gurkhas decided to remain on the strategic defensive and fight on their home territory, hitherto thought impregnable. The British organized an expeditionary force of some 22,000 men divided into four divisions, with a

British progress in the Nepal War was seriously hampered by the nature of the Nepalese terrain, the tactically astute Gurkhas having fortified the major positions with soundly-built and well-sited forts such as the one illustrated.

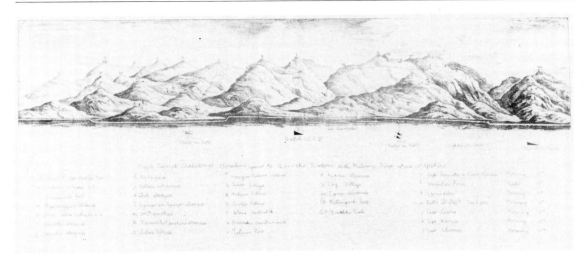

The type of terrain in which the Gurkhas lived and by preference fought is well illustrated by this contemporary sketch of the Gurkha defences faced at Maloun by Major General Ochterlony's force on 14 and 15 April 1815.

garrison of 2700 men left for the defence of the border region east of the Coosy river.

The tenor of the whole campaign was set by the first action, in which one of the British divisions had to take the hill fortress of Kalunga, which was garrisoned by some 600 Gurkhas. Under the personal command of Major General Rollo Gilespie the British first assaulted the fortress frontally and were repulsed with considerable losses. Gilespie was killed. More sensible tactics then prevailed, and Kalunga was taken under siege by an artillery bombardment. The effects of this large-scale bombardment eventually persuaded the Gurkhas to pull back, but not before further losses had been inflicted on the British. So stout a defence had not been anticipated (and indeed not been experienced by the British in India for some time), and caused the divisional commanders to act with extreme caution thereafter. The one exception was Major General David Ochterlony, who refused to allow sensible caution to become outright lack of decision. Local tribes were persuaded to throw in their lot with the British, and Ochterlony's division reinforced the tribes' morale by pressing on against the Gurkhas, under the personal command of Umur Sing, with unswerving determination. The division pushed on into the Nepalese hinterland, reducing several im-

portant hill fortresses as it went, and eventually pinned Umur Sing at a position at Maloun after a series of skilfully executed manoeuvres which the Gurkhas were unable to counter. The Maloun position was naturally strong, consisting of a line of fortified hilltops along a ridge projecting into the Sutlej river, and it could be expected that the British would face determined and capable opposition: the memory of Kalunga was still strong, for although the Gurkhas had lost 520 out of 600 defenders at this position, they had inflicted grievous losses before pulling out.

While Ochterlony's division had been pressing the Gurkhas' central force under Umur Sing, other British divisions had been making steady progress into Kumaon, and after a series of actions had driven the Gurkhas out of their favourite hilltop fortifications, the capture of the Setoli heights unseamed the entire Gurkha hold on Kumaon, which fell into British hands.

Ochterlony was also pushing ahead with the reduction of the entire Maloun position: the Ryla peak was taken without Gurkha opposition, but the capture of the second peak, Deothul, was achieved on 15 April 1815 only after a strenuous and costly action. The British immediately set about strengthening the Gurkha defences with additional earthworks, but a violently determined Gurkha counterattack on the next day very nearly succeeded in ousting the British: the Gurkhas managed to penetrate into the British position in several breakthroughs, and it was only as a result of the arrival of reinforcements from the Ryla peak that the Gurkha counterattack was contained and thrown back. British respect for the capabilities of the individual Gurkha had already been raised to a formidable degree by the defence of Kalunga, but the utmost determination and courage of the counterattack at Deothul raised it yet further. The British placed great reliance on their artillery, and the astute Gurkhas had readily appreciated the fact that effective field artillery gave the British a decisive advantage. During the counterattack, therefore, the artillery received a deluge of fire, and at one stage there survived only one officer and three men to serve the guns. After the defeat of the Gurkha counterattack at Deothul it was reckoned that the British had suffered 213 casualties to the Gurkhas' 500 dead.

At this point the news of the Gurkha loss of Kumaon reached the Maloun position, seriously disheartening the Gurkha garrison at Maloun, one of the two principal flanking features in the whole position. Despite the objections of Umur Sing,

A contemporary illustration highlights the type of terrain over which the British and Nepalese fought in the Nepal War. This is the scene of the final operations of 25 April 1815, when the British forces commanded by Colonel Nicholls secured Kumaon province.

therefore, the Gurkhas at Maloun capitulated, leaving Umur Sing with a strength of only about 250 diehard supporters. Whatever else his failings, Umur Sing was a realist, and seeing that further resistance to the British was futile he and his supporters surrendered. The British now declared Nepal to be under British protection, returned captured lands to their owners, and offered the Nepalese peace under the terms of a treaty.

Quite extraordinarily, the Nepalese government refused to accept the peace treaty, which had been drawn up by Moira's successor as Governor General of Bengal, Lord Hastings. Further conflict was therefore inevitable, and in January 1816 Ochterlony, who had been knighted for his part in the previous year's campaign, led a British force of 17,000 men against the Nepalese. The Gurkhas had taken advantage of the lull in which peace had been discussed to renew their capabilities, and Ochterlony was little surprised to find that virtually the entire length of the Dun hills had been fortified to prevent any incursion from the south. Ochterlony made the eminently sensible decision not to divide his forces, but rather to strike in a cohesive and overwhelming strength straight for a decisive point: the British scouts reported a way of turning the Gurkha defensive line by means of a tortuous ravine

The man who raised the Kumaon Battalion, the kernel from which sprang the 3rd Gurkha Rifles of later years, was Sir Robert Colquhoun.

Military leader of the Nepalese in their war with the British, Umur Sing was the brother of the Nepalese prime minister and a capable commander.

through the hills, and Ochterlony was thus able to spear straight up the valley of the Raptie river towards Mukwanpur, brushing aside a number of Gurkha secondary positions as he advanced. The British progress had the desired effect of compelling the Gurkhas into a general engagement, in which British discipline, artillery and numbers inevitably triumphed. The Nepalese government was forced to accede to the terms of Hastings' treaty, and peace returned to this troubled area with the signature of the Treaty of Sagauli in 1816, which stripped Nepal of the Terai and imposed a British Resident on the authorities in Katmandu.

There never existed during the next 40 or so years anything more than a nominal friendship between the Nepalese government and the British administration of Bengal, but far more important ties had been forged at a lower level during the bitter battles of the previous two years, in which the British and Gurkhas had each come to a deep appreciation of the other's military virtues. This feeling is perhaps best encapsulated in two small episodes from the campaign of 1814, one from each side of the lines. In the first, the British erected at Kalunga a small monument to the Gurkhas who had defended the position so tenaciously; on the obelisk was inscribed the legend: 'They fought in their conflict like men and, in the intervals of actual conflict, showed us a liberal courtesy.' In the second instance, a party of irregulars led by Lieutenant Frederick Young was surprised by a force of Gurkhas and decamped, leaving the British officers to face the Gurkhas alone; his captors were amazed that Young and his subordinates had not also fled, and on being told that 'I have not come so far in order to run away. I came to stay.' replied that 'We could serve under men like you.'

Young now became a key figure in the promotion of Gurkha interests under the British flag, for during the armistice in 1815 pending the treaty negotiations he proposed that a corps of Gurkha soldiers be raised to serve in the army of the Honourable East India Company. Young's experience with the courage of the Gurkhas was extensive: General Gilespie had died in his arms at Kalunga, and later in the battle Young was amazed to see a Gurkha indicating that he wished to parley with the British; what he wanted was medical attention for his ruined jaw, after which he requested permission to return to his own lines to continue the action.

Young was given permission to raise a Gurkha corps, and his success is well attested in his own words: 'I went there one man and came out three thousand.' Not surprisingly, such a move could hardly find favour with the Nepalese government, but a formal agreement was signed whereby 'All the troops in the service of Nepal, with the exception of those granted to the personal honour of Kagjees Ummersing and Rangor Sing, will be at liberty to enter into the services of the British Government if agreeable to themselves and the British government choose to accept their services.' Notwithstanding the tacit disapproval of Katmandu, Gurkhas from the hill tribes flocked to the British colours. Some were men captured in the fighting, and others were hill tribesmen to whom glowing reports of the British

had been relayed. During 1815, therefore, four local battalions of Gurkhas were raised: the 1st Nusseree (Nasiri) Battalion, the 2nd Nusseree (Nasiri) Battalion, the Sirmoor Battalion, and the Kemaon (Kumaon) Provincial Battalion. The first three were Gurkha regiments from Nepal, and the last a battalion of Kumaonis and Garhwalis from the regions stripped from Nepal, and intended only for provincial duties. It is worth noting at this stage that during their lifetimes, current and extinct Gurkha regiments have undergone a bewildering number of designation alterations. Some of the more significant are mentioned in the body of the book, but a full list of all the regiments with their varying designations is contained in an appendix at the end of the book.

One of the factors that emerged almost immediately after the raising of these battalions was the enthusiasm of the men, which allowed rapid progress with training. Young, who served as commander of the Sirmoor Battalion for 28 years, was able to report his battalion ready for service within six

A Gurkha sepoy is seen in the dress typical of about 1816, with native shoes, blue trousers with the kukri at the front, green tunic with black facings and lace, and a small round black cap.

By the 1820s the uniform of the Gurkhas had evolved somewhat, as this illustration of men from the 1st Nasiri (Sabathu) Battalion testifies. The predominant colour is rifle green, with black facings and accoutrements, while the shako is black. The kukri was probably worn on the right hip.

months of its formation. But it was not until 1817 that the first of the Gurkha battalions was to see active service under the British flag, in this instance during the Mahratta War. In this small war the British forces commanded by Ochterlony were able to outmanoeuvre the rebellious Mahrattas and Pindaris and bring them to their senses before any major bloodshed was necessary. Only in one place, Sambhar, was a major action fought, and here the Sirmoor Battalion played a useful part in the Reserve Division's overrunning of the position. As a reward Ochterlony gave the battalion the honour of escorting to Delhi the 300 Mahratta guns captured or surrendered in the campaign.

The year 1823 saw the first of the designation changes that have at times made it difficult to follow the career of individual battalions. In this year the 1st and 2nd Nusseree Battalions became the 5th and 6th Local Battalions, while the Sirmoor Battalion became the 8th Local Battalion and the Kumaon Battalion, the 9th Local Battalion. It should be noted, moreover, that the numbers of Gurkhas in British service had been growing steadily: in 1817 there had been formed the Fatehgarh Legion and

Cuttack Legion, which eventually became the 9th and 6th Gurkha Rifles in the definitive expression of the Gurkha regiments' nomenclature. And it is worth noting at this stage that the 1st Nusseree Battalion eventually became the 1st Gurkha Rifles, the 2nd Nusseree Rifles were disbanded in 1830, the Sirmoor Rifles finally emerged as the 2nd Goorkha Rifles, and the Kumaon Battalion was in its ultimate form the 3rd Gurkha Rifles.

Further expansion took place in 1824 with the raising of the Sylhet Local Battalion, later the 1st Battalion, 8th Gurkha Rifles. The 2nd Battalion, 8th Gurkha Rifles, came into being during 1835 as the Assam Sebundy Corps. But this is to jump ahead chronologically, for in 1824 the Gurkhas saw their second taste of action when the 8th Local Battalion was sent in against a Goojar rising in the eastern Dun region. Summoned by the magistrate at Saharanpur, Young and a force of 200 Gurkhas force-marched 36 miles from their station at Dehra Dun to the rebel base at Koonja within the day and decisively beat a force of some 800 rebels, who had been so confident of victory that they had engaged the Gurkhas outside the relative safety of their large mud-built fort. The survivors of the engagement promptly took refuge inside the fort, however, leaving Young with a nasty tactical problem: delay would permit the rebels to filter away for a later reunification, while an immediate assault was made difficult by the Gurkhas' lack of ladders or other siege equipment. The problem was exacerbated by the fact that Young's Gurkhas were outnumbered by about three-to-one by the rebels in the fort. Young reasoned that the only realistic access to the fort was through the wooden gates which, in the absence of engineers, artillery or even gunpowder, could only be breached by a battering ram. Thus an improvised ram was devised by the cutting down and trimming of a large tree, to be carried on a rope cradle. The rest of Young's tactical plan had to be simple: while the battering ram was used against the gate, part of the Gurkha force would provide covering fire while the remainder remained poised to pour through any breach. Casualties were high, but the plan worked: after five blows the Goojars' gate collapsed, and Young led his men into the fort, which fell after some 150 Goojars had been killed in hand-to-hand fighting. Since that time the battalion (and successor regiment) has worn a ram's head on regimental accoutrements.

Of the new units, the first into action was the Cuttack Legion, which was in fact hardly a true Gurkha battalion at all until 1828. It was only in this year that the first Gurkhas from Nepal were recruited, and then they formed only two of the battalion's 10 companies. (The battalion became wholly Gurkha, albeit under a radically altered title, in 1886.) However, whatever its origins the battalion was soon in action, initially against rebellious Kol tribesmen in the Cuttack region. Little is known of the Cuttack Legion's specific actions in this short campaign, but after its termination the Cuttack Legion was moved to Rangpur in Bengal, where the unit became the Rangpur Light Infantry Battalion and played its part in the 1st Burma War (1824–1826), which was sired by a period of active and tactically efficient Burmese expansion.

In 1819 the Burmese had conquered Assam, and substantial numbers of Assamese refugees fled over the border into Manipur, which was under British protection. But from Manipur the refugees instigated a guerrilla war against the Burmese, who complained in vain to the Honourable East India Company about the situation. By 1823 the governor of Assam, the excellent general Maha Bandula, had lost all patience with the Honourable East India Company's total inaction on the matter and decided to resolve the situation to Burma's military advantage. In 1823, therefore, Maha Bandula launched a two-part offensive against Bengal from Assam and Arakan, the Burmese having already overrun Manipur and Cachar against wholly inadequate British and local forces. The Burmese were soon in a position to threaten the major port and city of Chittagong with their advance from Assam, and it was in the blunting of this attack, which spurred the British declaration of war in March 1824, that the Rangpur Light Infantry Battalion first entered the fray. The war continued with a series of British offensives up to the end of 1825, when the British threat to the Burmese capital of Ava persuaded the Burmese to capitulate in February 1826. The Rangpur Light Infantry Battalion played a useful but relatively undistinguished part in these operations, losing a few men to the usual assortment of combat reasons, but a far larger number to the assorted diseases prevalent in the Burmese river valleys up which the majority of the fighting was launched.

The Treaty of Yandabo that ended the 1st Burma War saw a Burmese cession of several areas to the British. Among these was Assam, and to this region was posted the Rangpur Light Infantry Battalion, which had in 1826 been redesignated the 8th (Rangpur) Local Light Infantry Battalion; the change of base led to a further designation change, this time to the 8th (Assam) Local Light Infantry Battalion from 1828; the move to Assam was also accompanied by the addition of two wholly Gurkha companies to the battalion. Based at Sadiya, the battalion was soon heavily involved in a bitter struggle with local Kachin hill peoples, especially those of the Singpoh tribe. Large numbers of small clashes took place, with the Gurkhas generally successful, but in 1839 a near-disaster overtook the battalion when the commanding officer, Lieutenant Colonel White, refused to accept that the Kampti tribe around Sadiya was planning to overrun the post. The attack fell on the British garrison at Sadiya in January 1839, and large numbers of soldiers as well as their dependants were killed, including White. But the battalion soon pulled itself together, and pursued the hostiles into the surrounding countryside. Here the Kamptis sought safety in dispersion, but with a ruthless determination the battalion hunted down the various small parties, killing many and capturing the rest. The tribe was then broken up into small units and dispersed into India proper.

The battalion became the 1st Assam Light Infantry in 1844, and its daily round continued to be the policing of this hostile corner of the Honourable East India Company's empire.

In the following year the battalion was again in action, this time during the campaign to oust the usurper Durjan Sal from the throne of Bhurtpore. The crisis had been triggered by the death of the previous rajah, Baldeo Sing, who left his throne to a younger son, Balwant Sing, under the regency of the boy's uncle. This rational arrangement was upset by Durjan Sal, a nephew of Baldeo Sing, who killed the uncle and his followers and imprisoned the young rajah. But Balwant Sing had already been recognized by the British as the rightful heir to Bhurtpore, and the defiance of Durjan Sal could not be allowed to set a precedent. The ever watchful Ochterlony prepared to move out swiftly against the rebels, but Lord Amherst forbade an early departure in the hope of solving the impasse by diplomatic means, a wish fostered by the heavy cost (in men and money) of the 1st Burma War and by unhappy reminders of the previous British assault upon Bhurtpore, which had failed with heavy losses. In the way of such matters, however, Durjan Sal inferred from the delay that the British were worried, and therefore became yet more truculent. Amherst, only recently arrived as Governor General of Bengal, at the end of 1825 finally realized that force was essential, and Lord Combermere was despatched with an expeditionary force of 21,000 men and 100 guns to deal with Durjan Sal, who had provisioned Bhurtpore admirably and built up a garrison of 25,000 Jats, Pathans and Rajputs. Among the British force were 100 men each from the 5th and 8th Local Battalions.

Despite the fact that the British delay had given Durjan Sal ample time to complete his defensive arrangements, the rapid arrival of the British force once hostilities had started prevented the beleaguered forces from flooding the moat that provided their outer defence line. Nonetheless, the fortress of Bhurtpore was a formidable obstacle, the walls being tall and extremely thick. Indeed, the strength of these fortifications defeated the efforts of the British artillery though they were built only of mud baked rock hard by the sun. The only recourse left to the British was mining, and the men of the two Gurkha battalions set to with a will in company with the rest of the troops. All was ready on 26 January 1826, and the Gurkhas were amongst the first through the breaches once the two mines were detonated. The garrison had been seriously demoralized by the two huge explosions, but the fighting was bitter: British casualties amounted to 600 while those of the defenders totalled some 14,000. Durjan Sal was captured and imprisoned, and Balwant Sing restored to his throne. Bhurtpore became the first battle honour of the 8th Local Battalion after the detachment at Bhurtpore had been praised highly by the divisional commander, Major General Nichols.

Further reorganization of the Gurkha force followed in 1826, when the 5th and 6th Local Battalions were amalgamated as the 4th Local Battalion. At the same time the 8th Local Battalion became the 6th (Sirmoor) Local Battalion and the 9th Local Battalion became the 7th (Kumaon) Local Battalion. There followed a period of some 20 years in which the peace of India was little disturbed, and the Gurkhas thus continued with the round of training and integration into the routines and organization of the army of the Honourable East India Company.

This peace could not and did not last, and in 1845 a serious problem arose with the Sikhs in the Punjab. It had long been appreciated by the British that this dynamic politico-religious regime could threaten British stability in the west of the country, but for some time the unrest in the Punjab had been checked by a leader of exceptional abilities, Ranjit Singh, 'the Lion of the Punjab'. Ranjit Singh was a man who thrived in the aura of intrigue and backstabbing prevalent in the Sikh region, but with his death in 1839 a ghastly power struggle erupted: Ranjit Singh's successor, Kurruck Singh, was soon murdered and his son, No Nehal Singh, was buried under a pile of bricks almost as his father's funeral was completed. The Punjab was embroiled in the most terrible wave of unrest and killing, though the one factor that preserved a measure of unity was fear that the British would intervene: the eminent soldier Sir Charles Napier had often prophesied that the British would inevitably have to move into the Punjab, and against the threat of such a British move a large Sikh army was prepared for an offensive strike across the Sutlej river. Given the conditions prevalent in the Punjab, these Sikh preparations took time and could hardly be concealed, giving the British the chance to muster a force of some 32,000 men and 68 guns at Ferozepur, Ludhiana and Umbala under the overall command of General Sir Hugh Gough.

The Sikh preparations were complete by the end of 1845, and the Sikh army swept across the Sutlej river on 11 December 1845, prompting a British declaration of war. By this time the two main British positions were the field-fortified sites at Ferozepur and Ferozshah. As news of the Sikh offensive revealed the true intentions and strength of the opposing force, a British column was despatched from Bussean to reinforce the position at Ferozepur. This detachment then became involved in the first battle of the 1st Sikh War, the Battle of Mudki, when news of a Sikh force in the vicinity was received on 18 December. The 1200 men of the British column set off on that date to try to reach Ferozepur, but were intercepted in the late afternoon by the Sikhs. A short but savage engagement followed, the Sikhs being repulsed with heavy casualties and the loss of 17 guns. But the British had suffered terribly, losing 864 men, and could not follow up their tactical advantage in this first battle.

Thus the scene was set for the first major engagement, the Battle of Ferozshah on 21 December 1845. The British were commanded by Gough, who had as his second-in-command Sir Henry Harding, Governor General of Bengal, who had nonetheless volunteered to serve militarily under Gough. The British totalled 18,000 men and 65 guns, and after a dispute between Gough and Harding, this force fell upon the Sikhs (numbering some 35,000 men with 85 guns under Lal Singh) late in the afternoon. Nightfall prevented the full development of the battle, though the British conducted a night assault to spike the Sikh guns that were cannonading their lines to good effect. Early on the following day the British attacked the Sikh position yet again, and after a bloody battle secured the victory and 76 guns. However, losses on both sides had been heavy: the Sikhs lost at least 10,000 men, and the British losses of some 2400 men prevented Gough from pursuing the Sikhs as they pulled back towards Lahore to regroup and reassess their strategy.

As the British awaited reinforcements, the Sikhs yet again moved onto the offensive, building a pontoon bridge across the Sutlej river to establish a potent bridgehead at Sobraon, while another Sikh force rapidly developed a useful fortified position at Aliwal in the region of Ludhiana. The local commander was General Sir Harry Smith, an officer of considerable ability, and his forces included elements of two Gurkha battalions, the 4th (Nasiri) Rifle Battalion and the 6th (Sirmoor) Local Battalion. Smith moved with considerable speed, and after a small engagement with the Sikh forces under Runjoor Singh on 21 January 1846 relieved Ludhiana. Refusing to pause, Smith then swept on to Aliwal, where the main Sikh force under Runjoor Singh was concentrated. Like that for Ferozshah,

the Battle of Aliwal was one of the most viciously fought actions ever seen on Indian soil: Smith launched his attack with a brief but concentrated artillery bombardment on the Sikh positions, after which the 16th Lancers were sent in with infantry support. The fighting was bitter in the extreme, and at one stage the 6th (Sirmoor) Local Battalion lost its colours and then recaptured them. The Sikhs were decisively beaten and pulled back across the Sutlej river.

Smith again pressed on, marching via Ferozepur to Sobraon, where the Sikhs had used their time to full advantage in the construction of a massive field fortification to supplement the natural strength of their position in a bend of the river. Estimates have put the strength of the Sikhs at between 50,000 and 54,000 men with 70 guns, while the British force, under the overall command of Gough once again, totalled some 16,000 men with 99 guns. This artillery superiority stood the British in good stead, for after a massive bombardment on 10 February 1846 Gough's forces stormed into the breached fortifications for another costly hand-to-hand battle with the Sikhs, who were again decisively beaten. Yet again, however, the butcher's bill was prodigious: the Battle of Sobraon cost the victors 2383 casualties, while those of the vanquished were at least 10,000 men. The Sikhs also lost 67 guns, and this crushing reverse finally persuaded the Sikhs that further resistance was futile. The two Gurkha battalions played a useful part in the Battle of Sobraon, and were part of the British force that pushed on to Lahore, where the Treaty of Lahore was signed on 11 March 1846 to end the war and make the Punjab a British protectorate.

Nothing in the 1st Sikh War had persuaded the Sikhs to alter their basic feelings about the British, however, and despite their losses the Sikhs could take considerable pride in the performance of their troops in action against the British. Thus the Punjab remained in a state of considerable ferment, needing only the right accident of fortune to trigger renewed hostilities. The trigger was an incident at Multan on 20 April 1848, in which two British officers were murdered. It was clear that punitive measures must follow, and the Sikhs decided to strike first, though the Sikh authorities at first tried to stem the rising before deciding to capitalize on the strength of Sikh feeling and so changing sides. Thus started the 2nd Sikh War after the defection of the Sikh government in August.

Operations began with a British initiative, when during November 1848 the Sikh fortress of Multan was taken under siege by a detachment of the main British forces under the command of General William Whish, subordinate to Gough as commander-in-chief. The 2nd Sikh War followed the same basic pattern as the 1st Sikh War, with the Sikhs generally content to remain on the tactical defensive behind earthwork fortifications and masses of artillery. Despite a serious reverse at the Battle of Chillianwalla in January 1849, the British were generally successful, and brought the war to a successful conclusion with the crushing of the main Sikh army (with Afghan support) at the Battle of Gujerat in February 1849. No Gurkha battalions were involved in the 2nd Sikh War, though the subsequent annexation of the Punjab, into the British imperial holdings in India resulted in the formation of the Punjab Frontier Force, which included from 1858 the Hazara Goorkha Battalion, which finally became the 5th Gurkha Rifles.

It is perhaps worth amplifying the part played by the two Gurkha battalions in the subjugation of the Punjab. At Aliwal, for example, the 6th (Sirmoor) Battalion was on the left of the British line as part of General Wheeler's brigade, which was heavily engaged by the Sikh artillery. In the savage hand-to-hand fighting that followed the arrival of Wheeler's brigade in the Sikh positions, the battalion's colours were severely rent by the amount of metal in the air, the officer carrying them was killed, and the Sikhs managed to make off with them. However, a party rallied by Havildar Badalsing Thapa swept through into the Sikh position to recapture the colours and also to seize a Sikh standard. This proved a decisive moment in the Battle of Aliwal, and from this point

the Sikhs began to lose heart. The battalion's part in the victory was crucial, but the 6th (Sirmoor) Local Battalion in the process lost some 50 men from the British total of about 590.

This same battalion also played an important part in the Battle of Sobraon, where its commander, Captain Fisher, was killed. The Sirmoor Battalion was this time in the centre of the British line as part of the division commanded by General Gilbert, and suffered losses in proportion to its principal role. The battle was described by Smith as a 'brutal bulldog fight', and among the British losses were numbered some 100 men of the Sirmoor Battalion. Gough later wrote of the Gurkhas that while they were 'Soldiers of small stature, but indomitable spirit, they vied in ardent courage with the Grenadiers of our own nation, and armed with a short weapon of their own country, were a terror to the Sikhs . . .'

The Gurkha battalions were soon able to return to their peacetime routines, although unrest continued in the Punjab as a result of governmental parsimony: with the annexation of the Punjab the previous 'overseas' allowance for the troops was discontinued with relatively little benefit to the treasury but considerable disaffection amongst the 25 regiments destined for service in the Punjab. The one regiment actually to mutiny was the 66th Bengal Native Infantry, but this was rapidly broken by the 1st Native Cavalry. The mutineers were immediately despatched to Ambala for the disbandment of the regiment. The escort was found by the 4th (Nasiri) Rifle Battalion, which was in 1850 taken into the body of the Honourable East India Company's line regiments as the 66th or Goorkha Regiment, Bengal Native Infantry. In this new guise it received additional pay, being regular rather than irregular infantry, and the added prestige of a line regiment.

Sir Jang Bahadur Rana, prime minister of Nepal.

THE
INDIAN
MUTINY

Though considerable success had attended the efforts of British arms during the various Indian wars of the first half of the 19th century, not all was well with the Bengal Army of the Honourable East India Company. The reasons for and progress of this disastrous state of affairs are beyond the scope of this book, but came to a head in 1857 with the issue of a new Enfield rifle, a considerable improvement over the muskets hitherto used by the majority of British and Indian troops. Nobody objected to the new weapon, but rumblings of discontent almost immediately started about the cartridge to go with it, for rumour had it that this was greased with a mixture of fats from animals objectionable to both the Moslems and the Hindus who formed the vast majority of the 263,000 natives amongst the 300,000 troops in India. To Moslems the biting open of such a cartridge would entail defilement, and to a Hindu a loss of caste that could only be redeemed through costly and time-consuming purification. The matter of the cartridges has never been adequately resolved, but it provided just the right trigger for the combination of grievances hitherto endured by the Indian sepoys. Various rumblings of serious disaffection had previously been papered over, but in March 1857 Sepoy Mangal Pande of the 34th Native Infantry tried to urge his fellow soldiers to mutiny, and then wounded a British officer who tried to arrest him. Pande was later tried and executed for mutiny, and this sparked off the Indian Mutiny, undoubtedly the greatest threat there ever was to the continuance of British rule in India. The real start of the mutiny may be dated to 10 May 1857, when the Meerut garrison rebelled and was joined by the mob from Delhi in an orgy of looting and destruction. Delhi was in the hands of the mutineers on 11 May, and the Moghul emperor had been elevated as the titular head of the rebellion. The British position was parlous in the extreme, a number of British regiments having been drafted out to the Crimean War without replacement, but the situation was saved somewhat by the steadfast loyalty of a number of native regiments, including the Gurkhas.

There were at this time seven Gurkha battalions: the 66th or Goorkha Regiment, Bengal Native Infantry; the Sirmoor Battalion; the 7th (Kumaon) Local Battalion; the 1st Assam Light Infantry Regiment; the 11th (Sylhet) Local Light Infantry

Battalion; the 63rd Regiment, Bengal Native Infantry; and a Gurkha battalion in the Corps of Guides. In the panic-struck early stages of the mutiny there were rumours that the 66th had mutinied and was threatening Simla from its base at Jutogh, but these rumours were soon revealed as baseless. In fact the only instance of trouble with a Gurkha unit occurred at Kussowlie, where a small group of Gurkhas robbed the treasury and ran amok. Sense prevailed amongst the British command, who appreciated that the summary elimination of this small group could achieve little other than the alienation of other Gurkhas. So nothing more than defensive precautions were undertaken by the 75th Foot at Simla, General George Anson, the British commander-in-chief then sending one Captain Briggs to the troublesome Gurkhas with an offer of pardon if they returned to obedience. This was just what was needed, and the trouble soon passed without further fears for the steadfast loyalty of the Gurkhas.

Delhi was the main centre of the uprising, and it was clear from the earliest days of the mutiny that if the British were to overcome what was in essence a rising by certain elements of the Bengal Army, with widespread civilian support only in Oudh, Delhi must first be contained as a hostile military centre, and then recaptured. It was estimated that the mutinous soldiers in Delhi numbered some 20,000, with reinforcements arriving fairly regularly, and that the city also contained vast quantities of armaments as well as being the capital of the titular head of the rising, Bahadur Shah.

Only some 2000 to 3000 British troops could initially be raised to begin the containment of Delhi, and command was made all but impossible by a serious outbreak of cholera, which killed a suc-

The Maharajah Sir Jang Bahadur Rana, GCB, CCST lived from 1817 to 1877, and was both prime minister and commander-in-chief during a turbulent period of history on the Indian subcontinent, but proved a staunch and capable ally of the British.

Sir Jang Bahadur Rana was prime minister of Nepal at the time of the Indian Mutiny, and immediately offered the British 6000 Nepalese soldiers as reinforcements, later taking the field with his men to participate in the siege of Lucknow. Throughout the mutiny, the Nepalese fought alongside the British and suffered heavy casualties in support of their allies.

cession of senior officers. Nevertheless the British advance from Umballa (Ambala) towards Delhi began in the middle of May under the immediate command of Brigadier General Wilson's Delhi Field Force, which included the Sirmoor Battalion and the 7th (Kumaon) Local Battalion. The only other Gurkha unit to be involved in the Indian Mutiny was the 1st Assam Light Infantry, which remained

on garrison duty and helped keep the peace in the Chittagong region after moving from Dibrugarh.

The battalion which immortalized itself was the Sirmoor Battalion, which had the distinction of being the only unit of the Delhi Field Force to remain in the line for the whole period of the siege of Delhi, a period of three months and eight days. The siege was at first dominated by the total imbalance of the forces involved, and the British therefore decided to seize the Delhi ridge running north of the city rather than to try the impossible task of investing a powerful position with a circumference of about 7 miles. The British plan was then to develop the ridge position as an effective base for further operations, invite and crush any attacks from Delhi, and to await reinforcement before attempting to capture Delhi. The Delhi Field Force was able to take this Badli-ki-Serai ridge on 8 June after a sharp action lasting some 2 hours. At the heart of the action was the Sirmoor Battalion commanded by Major Charles Reid, which had started its advance from Dehru Dun on 14 May via Meerut. The battalion had already encountered several parties of mutineers, who had been seriously handled when they resisted; any captured ringleaders were summarily tried and executed in front of a firing squad without any difficulty from co-religious Gurkhas. During the subsequent march on Delhi, a prodigious feat in the middle of summer and during a virulent outbreak of disease, the Sirmoor Battalion first met the 60th Rifles, beginning a close association that was to last somewhat over a century. The first meeting was hardly auspicious, however, for the Gurkhas were bivouacked under the guns of the Delhi Field Force's artillery, which had orders to destroy the battalion should any signs of mutiny be detected.

Suspicion of the Gurkhas' true loyalty lasted no longer than the first day that the British forces were on Delhi ridge: the mutineers launched a spirited counterattack on the British position during the afternoon of 8 June, and the Sirmoor Battalion was at the centre of the defence together with two companies of the 60th Rifles and a battery of artillery. The action raged for 16 hours before the mutineers were pushed back to the city walls, and the conspicuous part played by the Sirmoor Battalion permitted no further suspicion about Gurkha loyalty to the British cause, and the Gurkhas were

rewarded by being made the main picket for the Delhi Field Force with its base around the hotly disputed Hindu Rao's House. Reid was clearly an able tactician, and though his position suffered on a permanent basis from an incessant artillery barrage from the mutineers' positions (as close as 1200 yards to the Gurkhas' main line), Reid was not content to remain on the tactical defensive: raids were launched into the mutineers' lines, and whenever he saw that an assault was being prepared, Reid launched his own forces in a pre-emptive raid to disrupt the mutineers' preparations. Thus, though the Gurkhas and supporting riflemen were hopelessly outnumbered, they more than counterbalanced this factor by their tactical superiority and aggressive patrolling. Losses were inevitably heavy, and by the end of June the Sirmoor Battalion had lost 138 out of 490 men. Reinforcements were sent from Dehra Dun, but these did not arrive until the end of July, and the main picket was augmented by additional riflemen (60th Rifles and Coke's Rifles) and men of the Guides Corps.

While Reid's force held and blunted the mutineers' offensive ambitions, the British command was under increasing pressure for an outright assault on Delhi to end the siege. But Wilson was sensibly cautious about such a move as he fully appreciated the basic strength of the mutineers' position and the comparative weakness of the British force, especially in artillery (for large portions of the Delhi ridge 'campaign', the British had been so short of artillery shot that they had been forced to scavenge and use battered rounds fired by the mutineers). By August the British forces had increased to some 8000 men with an adequate force of heavy artillery, and Wilson began his plans for an assault on Delhi during September. Thus the mutineers' last throw came on 30 August, when the Delhi ridge was assaulted by a substantial force from the mutineers' Delhi strength

The Sirmoor Battalion parades in the Subzee Mundee suburb of Delhi before moving onto Delhi Ridge for the defence of the Hindu Rao's House.

Men of the Sirmoor Battalion parade in front of the Hindu Rao's House on Delhi Ridge, scene of their superb defence during the direst days of the Indian Mutiny. As can be seen, the house was badly damaged in the almost incessant fighting for this key spot.

of about 40,000. The importance of this attack was fully appreciated by the mutineers, and the attack was watched from the city walls by Bahadur Shah, who had promised 10 rupees for every British and Gurkha head brought back by the attackers. That they were rated as highly as the British by the mutineers was a great and justified compliment to the Gurkhas. This last attack was again a bitterly contested affair, and in Reid's words 'The rascals found me at home and took a sound thrashing.'

Extract·from·General Orders·by·H.E·the·Commander in·Chief· 27ᵗʰ February 1850.

The Native Officers, non-commissioned Officers and Private Sepoys of the 66ᵗʰ regiment are to be marched to Umballah, and there struck off from the service of the Honorable East India Company, and His Excellency directs that the colours of the 66ᵗʰ are to be delivered over to the brave and loyal men of the ████ussereet ████oorka battalion and that the 66ᵗʰ regiment shall in future be denominated the ████ or ████oorka ████egiment

In 1850 the 66th Regiment of Bengal Native Infantry, a Gurkha battalion, was so incensed at official parsimony at the reduction of 'overseas' allowances that it mutinied and attempted to seize Govidghur, which was generally believed to hold a large treasure. The mutiny was put down by the 1st Native Cavalry and the 66th disbanded at Ambala (Umballa), its place being taken by the 4th (Nasiri) Rifle Battalion which had escorted the 66th to Ambala.

The British assault on Delhi was to be supported by 60 pieces of heavy artillery, which were to conduct a three-day bombardment of the walls before the assault force was sent in. This assault force, commanded by Brigadier General John Nicholson, was organized as four columns and comprised some 4000 men in all. One of the columns was commanded by Reid and mustered about 2500 men of the Sirmoor Battalion (only 200 men), parties of the 60th Rifles, the 61st and 75th Foot, Coke's Rifles and Tomb's Troop of the Royal Horse Artillery. This British assault was to mark the end of the siege of Delhi, in which the Gurkhas had already distinguished themselves at very considerable cost. But there was to be no respite for the Sirmoor Battalion, for Reid's column was to spearhead the British advance, the column's central progress being designed to mask the movement of the main forces on the flanks and from the rear. The actual attack of the Gurkhas' column was led by Captain Lawrence, Major Reid having been wounded in the head just as

the final preparations for the assault were being completed. This resulted in a slight delay, which unmasked the other columns and reduced the tactical surprise achieved as the assault went in in the very early morning of 14 September. Nicholson was killed as the assault force stormed into the breached walls against fanatical resistance from the mutineers, but once the British were inside the walls the outcome was little in doubt. Three days of the most savage fighting followed before the mutineers' main resistance was broken, and pockets of sepoys were finally overwhelmed in the next three days. Remembering the mutineers' massacre of British troops and civilians at Cawnpore earlier in the rebellion, the attackers were regrettably short of mercy, and horrendous casualties were inflicted on the mutineers and civilians of Delhi. Bahadur Shah was captured, his sons were shot, and the city was most severely handled. Reid's column was again one of the forces that took most casualties, which amounted to 1574 amongst the attacking force. During its lengthy sojourn in the line the Sirmoor Battalion suffered total casualties of 370 men out of an original total of 490.

Although less heavily engaged, the 7th (Kumaon) Local Battalion also played a notable part in the siege of Delhi, especially in its closing stages. The battalion was heavily engaged during the preparations for the artillery barrage that was to precede the actual assault, initially by distracting the fire of the mutineers' artillery that might otherwise have been able to engage in counterbattery fire, and then in protecting the guns from the attentions of enemy raids. Then the battalion was involved in the storming of Delhi, being part of the column commanded by Sir Colin Campbell. Nicholson led the whole assault with this column, and was mortally wounded during the assault on the Kashmir Gate, where the 7th (Kumaon) Local Battalion especially distinguished itself.

There can be no question of the fact that the most distinguished part in the entire siege was played by the Sirmoor Battalion. Thus the Gurkhas came to play a decisive role in history, for with the loss of Delhi and the capture of Bahadur Shah the mutiny was fated: there was still a ghastly amount of fighting to be done, but the loss of Delhi put the writing on the wall for the mutineers and put an end to any dreams of a revival of the Moghul empire. Honours were heaped on the battalion: Reid was promoted to colonel; the battalion was with the 60th Rifles sent to garrison the key Red Fort, and was awarded the unique distinction of a third colour inscribed with the word Delhi, and with the wholehearted approval of the 60th Rifles, the battalion was turned into a rifle unit. This was confirmed in 1858 when the Sirmoor Battalion became the Sirmoor Rifle Regiment, and its uniform included the scarlet facings of the 60th Rifles. Even after it had become a rifle regiment, which generally carried no colours, the Sirmoor Rifle Regiment retained the unusual distinction of its three colours until 1861, when the regiment was taken into the regular establishment of the new British army in India, and thereby lost the right to colours. As a mark of her special favour, Queen Victoria sent the regiment a silver truncheon to be carried by the native officer who had hitherto carried the third colour, and to be awarded the same honours as a colour.

It should also be noted that an important part in

A group of men and NCOs of the Nasiri Rifle Battalion, together with a British officer, pose for the camera in about 1850.

the mutiny was played by Gurkha troops of the Royal Nepalese army. Janbahadur Rana, the prime minister, offered the equivalent of some six battalions of Nepalese troops, 6000 men in all, and these were heavily engaged in the mopping-up operations in northern India, suffering relatively heavy casualties in the process. The Nepalese offer had been readily accepted because of the high reputation being won by the two battalions at Delhi, and Nepalese replacements for the men lost in northern India were eagerly accepted under the command of Janbahadur Rana himself. This force was finally absorbed into the British relief force that finally raised the mutineers' siege of Lucknow on 16 November 1857 under the command of Sir Colin Campbell. In recompense for their support during the mutiny, the Nepalese were given back the Terai region, and individual soldiers returned home well laden with booty.

Further evidence of the Gurkhas' loyalty in the mutiny is provided by the establishment of two more Gurkha battalions: the Hazara Goorkha Battalion has already been mentioned, and the other unit was the Extra Goorkha Regiment raised late in 1857 by Lieutenant MacIntyre. This latter eventually became the 4th Gurkha Rifles.

The Battle of Peiwar Kotal.

DUTY ON
TWO FRONTIERS

The Indian Mutiny had been a quite shattering experience for the British as well as for the Indians swept up in the turmoil that had engulfed Bengal and northern India. The cost in people had been high, the material and financial losses were severe, and the whole nature of British rule in India had been called into dispute and found wanting. It was inevitable, therefore, that the nature of British rule should be reassessed and modified to suit modern requirements and to remove the primary causes of the mutiny's origins.

The mutiny itself ended with the Battle of Gwalior in June 1858, and less than three months later, on 1 September 1858, the administration of India was taken over from the Honourable East India Company by the British crown. This administrative change could be effected moderately swiftly, but extensive thought and preparation had to be undertaken before the Honourable East India Company's three Indian armies (those of Bengal, Bombay and Madras) went the same way in 1861. Naturally enough, it was the Bengal army which had

The siege of the fortress of Chitral in 1882 brought a rapid response from the 2nd Goorkhas and the 3rd and 5th Gurkhas, and brought about the establishment of a fort at Malakand, commanding the southern approaches to Chitral. This latter fort was a home for the 4th Gurkhas until well into the 1930s. It is interesting to note that even areas as remote as Chitral could and did boast useful fortifications well able to handle infantry assaults without artillery support.

been most affected by the mutiny, and indeed it was reckoned that the Bengal Army had virtually ceased to exist: the 70 regular units on the establishment before the mutiny had been whittled down to a mere 16 after the mutiny, these being supported by a small number of irregular corps. In the short term numbers could be and were raised to respectable totals again by the incorporation into the regular establishment of the irregular corps that had distinguished themselves in circumstances where regular regiments had mutinied or been disbanded for fear of mutiny.

Already the Gurkhas were in something of an unusual position among the units in the Indian army, for ethnic and social differences had caused them to distance themselves from the Hindus of the north Indian plains. Like the Sikhs from the west, the Gurkhas felt a martial affinity with the British soldiers who had bested them, and even before the Sirmoor Battalion's classic performance on the Delhi ridge confirmed the superb fighting qualities of the Gurkhas there had begun to emerge a special relationship between the Gurkhas and the British. Perspicacious British officers had already come to appreciate this fact, for although the Gurkhas were an irregular corps (and thus denied the higher pay, special uniforms and even tents of the regular units) they felt that they were the equals of the British troops, and thus wished to be reckoned with them. This feeling stemmed in part from emotional reasons connected with the initial reasons for the

Gurkhas' loyalty to the British crown, but also in part from the disdain with which the high-caste Hindus of the regular regiments treated the Gurkhas, whom they considered low-caste and dirty folk from without the civilized world. Evidence of this tendency may be seen at the time that the Enfield rifle was introduced in 1857: four Gurkha detachments were sent to Ambala for training in the new weapons, and upon arrival these asked for permission to pitch their tents with the British soldiers rather than with the 'black folk'; and when issued with the ungreased cartridges specially prepared for the Indian regiments, the Gurkhas declined to use them, demanding instead the greased cartridges used by the British soldiers. Out of factors such as these grew the special relationship that slowly grew between the British officers and their Gurkha men, and between British and Gurkha regiments, fostered by the specific elitism of special units such as the Gurkhas and rifle regiments.

With the reorganization of the Indian army in 1861, the Gurkha regiments were taken onto the regular establishment. At the same time they were numbered on a separate roll, clearly presaging the

Good musketry, in terms of accuracy, fire discipline and speed of firing, has long been an attribute of the Gurkha rifleman. This photograph of men of the 2nd Goorkhas was taken during one of the interminable frontier campaigns that occupied the army in India during the last quarter of the nineteenth century, in this instance the Black Mountain campaign.

evolution of the Gurkhas as a force within but also separate from the other regiments of the Indian army. In this reorganization the 66th Goorkha Light Infantry Regiment became the 11th Regiment of Bengal Native Infantry and then the 1st Goorkha Regiment (Light Infantry) once the separate roll had been established; the Sirmoor Rifle Regiment became the 17th Regiment of Bengal Native Infantry and then the 2nd Goorkha (The Sirmoor Rifles) Regiment; the Kumaon Battalion became the 18th Regiment of Bengal Native Infantry and then the 3rd Goorkha Regiment; the Extra Goorkha Regiment became the 19th Regiment of Bengal Native Infantry and then the 4th Goorkha Regiment; and the Hazara Goorkha Battalion became the 7th Regiment of Infantry (Hazara Goorkha Battalion), Punjab Irregular Force and then the 5th Goorkha Regiment, or Hazara Goorkha Battalion. Of the other units with Gurkhas on the strength, the 1st Assam Light Infantry became the 46th Regiment of Bengal Native Infantry; the 11th or Sylhet Local (Light) Infantry Battalion became the 48th Regiment of Bengal Native Infantry and then the 44th Regiment of Bengal Native Infantry; the 63rd Regiment of Bengal Native Infantry became the 9th Regiment of Bengal Native Infantry; and the Assam Sebundy Corps became the 43rd Regiment of Bengal Native Infantry.

For the reorganized Indian army there was, perhaps fortunately, no lengthy period of inaction during which to recuperate but also to reiterate

previous grievances. India was beginning to settle relatively comfortably under the direct rule of the British, but the frontiers of that great country were still beset by innumerable small wars, campaigns and squabbles to keep the revived army fully occupied. Thus the North-West and North-East Frontiers of India came to play a decisive part in the development and growth of the Indian army, and of the Gurkha force within it. The causes of these intermittent but yet fairly continuous border conflicts were legion: traditional raiding by the hill tribes into the rich plains areas, inter-tribal conflict, religious fanaticism and, increasingly as the 19th century progressed, the effects of the 'Great Game' played between the United Kingdom and imperial Russia for the dominant influence in south central Asia. The effect on the Indian military establishment was the same no matter what the causes: a constant need to rotate fresh battalions to the frontier regions as a backstop for the local garrisons, with the result that there was a small but constant trickle of casualties (rising sharply in the case of more serious risings) but also an ideal training schedule to keep the battalions of the Indian army in the peak of tactical fitness for the special conditions prevailing.

In all this activity the Gurkhas played their normal capable but often superb part. It is impossible to cover, within the compass of a relatively short book, all the campaigns small and large which occupied this increasingly effective force, so mention will be made principally of the more interesting rather than necessarily more important campaigns.

First off the mark was the 1st Assam Light Infantry on the North-East Frontier, the year being 1858. The area had been ceded to the United Kingdom by the Burmese at the end of the 1st Burma War, and garrisons were immediately posted to the area, whose importance began to grow rapidly with the development of the tea trade from this seminal tea-growing region. The arrival of the Europeans and their troops was bad enough for the local tribes, but the fairly rapid erosion of their tribal lands for tea planting soon made matters worse.

However, in the short term the *casus belli* was the very presence of the British and the consequent disruption of the Assamese way of life as communications and trade began to reach into the area. Among the fiercest of the local tribes was the Abor, who in 1858 kicked over the traces and attacked a village near Dibrugarh, the base of the 1st Assam Light Infantry. An initial expedition against the tribesmen was a complete fiasco because of constant disagreement between the civil and military leaders, and the second proved successful in 1859 only because the colonel himself led the expedition with the support of Indian navy gunboats; nevertheless, some 45 casualties were suffered from the arrows of the Abors. The short campaign ended with the capture of the Abors' three main villages.

So far the 1st Assam Light Infantry contained a mere two companies of Gurkhas. But in 1864 this was increased, and an army order was issued dictating that the composition of the regiment should be mainly Gurkha and Assamese hillmen, with a maximum of 25 per cent Hindustanis. The regiment became wholly Gurkha in content only by 1886, when it was restyled the 42nd Regiment Goorkha Light Infantry. Even then there had been considerable dissension within the regiment, for the colonel wished to replace all Gurkhas with Sikhs, while most of the other officers wished to eliminate all Indians and Sikhs in favour of Gurkhas.

Other tribes who were a constant thorn in the side of the British were the Naga and Lushai, both of whom had long histories of tribal rivalry spattered with incidents of warfare and feuding. Given this history, both tribes were admirably versed in the tactics of guerrilla warfare in the terrain of Assam, and were able to keep constant pressure on the British garrisons in the area, with raids, attacks on outlying posts and the murder of workers in the tea plantations to keep the Gurkhas and other garrison regiments on their toes.

A photograph, probably taken in training, shows the service dress and kit of the 4th Gurkhas in about 1890. Note the practical tunic and the kukri scabbard on the right hip of the man with his back to the camera. The rifles are single-shot Martini-Henry weapons, which were introduced in 1871 and were slowly replaced by Lee-Metfords from 1888 onwards.

A considerable bond was formed between the Gurkhas and the Scots by various episodes, one of the most striking being the final bayonet charge by the 2nd Goorkhas and the 92nd Foot (The Gordon Highlanders) that helped to bring about the end of the 2nd Afghan War in 1879.

The Indian Army had long appreciated the value of drab uniform for low visibility in the irregular type of warfare waged on the North-West Frontier, and this lesson was forcibly drummed home to the British army by the Boer War. This Maxim machine-gun crew of Gurkha riflemen is seen on the North-West Frontier in 1906, the personal weapons being Lee Enfield rifles.

On occasion the daring and success of the tribesmen prompted the British to a punitive expedition, but all too often the local military authorities, with the support of the civil administration, hovered between a military ruthlessness and a laissez faire attitude. Thus the tribesmen did not know with any certainty what sort of retaliation their actions would provoke, but generally assumed that the British were too weak (both militarily and spiritually) to sustain a concerted military effort against the tribal unrest.

The Gurkhas were thus devoted for a period of some 50 years to garrison duties on this inhospitable frontier. Though less well known than the North-West Frontier, the North-East Frontier was no less troublesome and full of potential casualties for the garrison forces, though the terrain and the foe were markedly different from those of the North-West Frontier. In Assam the tribes were generally of moderate stature and generally not in possession of firearms. This latter should not be construed as a failing, however, for the weapons in widespread use were admirably suited to the tactics imposed upon the combatants by the terrain: thus spears, poisoned arrows and a wide variety of traps were as much feared by the British troops on the North-East Frontier as the long rifles of the Pathans and comparable tribesmen faced by the British troops on the North-West Frontier. The perpetual round of

operations on the North-East Frontier was a close-quarter type of fighting, and the troops had also to face far greater problems with disease than their opposite numbers on the North-West Frontier.

The Assamese peoples who perhaps gave the British the most trouble were the Lushais, who were implacably opposed to the dislocation of the area's status quo by the arrival of the British and the extensive development of tea plantations. Like the Nagas, the Lushais were fully at home in the humid and hilly jungles of the region, and over the centuries had established a way of life wholly in accord with local conditions. The key feature of this accommodation was the location of the Lushai villages on the tops of hills above the river valleys, where they enjoyed the benefits of sunshine and cooling breezes well removed from the steaming humidity and disease of the valleys proper. The natural defensive strength of these villages was enhanced by the tribal habit of throwing a palisade of sharpened bamboo stakes around the perimeter.

In 1871 the Lushais finally went too far, a large-scale raiding expedition getting almost as far as Cachar and in the process destroying several tea plantations, killing a number of local workers and destroying a couple of border posts. The authorities decreed that the time had come to deal the Lushais a decisive blow, in the hope that the lesson might deter further hostile action. A substantial force was thus divided into several columns that were to penetrate Lushai territory on what would now be called a 'seek and destroy' mission. Two Gurkha battalions were allocated to the expedition, the 42nd Regiment accompanying one column and the 2nd Goorkha Regiment forming part of the column that advanced into the southern portion of the Lushai area under the command of General Brownlowe.

The progress of the expeditionary column was relatively slow and beset by numerous ambushes and skirmishes, but for once a useful degree of intelligence preparation had been undertaken before the departure of the British force, and the columns closed in on the village of Lal Gnoora, known to be the leader of the most hostile Lushais. The village was finally achieved, and found to present formidable opposition to a force of infantry without artillery support as the position was encircled by belts of palisades some 8 or 9 ft high. The Lushais were well aware of the situation, and while the 2nd Goorkhas were pinned down as they deployed for a

The Chitral Expedition of 1895 again involved the Gurkhas, and the ponderous nature of such expeditions may be gauged from the extent and relative complexity of this tented encampment.

frontal assault on the village, the rest of Lal Gnoora's men set fire to the village as a distraction while the main Lushai force pulled out. The British impetus was preserved on the left flank, however, by Major McIntyre, who led his men over the palisades and into the burning village. Engaged from two quarters, the Lushais were heavily discomfited and broke away in confusion without inflicting on the Gurkhas' central companies the heavy losses that at one time seemed inevitable. McIntyre was awarded the Victoria Cross for his gallantry, which was instrumental in deciding the outcome of the campaign in favour of the Lushai Expeditionary Force: with Lal Gnoora's village destroyed on 4 January 1872, the British were able to push ahead more rapidly in the capture or reduction of other Lushai strongholds, so breaking the back of local resistance.

It is worth digressing at this point to mention 'The Charter', as a document issued by the government of India in 1864 is generally known. This paper

finally acceded to a point that had been raised on several occasions since the Gurkhas began to serve under the British flag: that they were volunteers who had left their own country to serve British interests, and that they therefore deserved more than a gratuity or the like at the end of their service, when they might be expected to return to Nepal. The truth of the case was ultimately agreed by the Indian government, and The Charter provided for the three regiments on the Bengal establishment (plus a fourth when it should be raised) to buy land and also to enjoy certain other privileges at the stations of Dharamsala (1st Gurkha Regiment), Dehra Dun (2nd Gurkha Regiment) and Almora (3rd Gurkha Regiment). Here Gurkha 'colonies' could thus be established, with obvious advantages to the ordinary Gurkha soldiers in terms of family, social background and retirement, and also easing the problem of recruitment, though there was little real difficulty with continued recruitment in Nepal, where hill Gurkhas were eager to join the colours. One of the principal successes of The Charter was that it

The inside of Chitral Fort is seen in 1895. Light field artillery was particularly important in frontier operations, but had to be light and handy for effective movement over inhospitable and extremely steep terrain.

permitted the Gurkha regiments to buy land in the region of their stations so that discharged soldiers could be allocated a small packet of land, so promoting the retention of old soldiers in the area of the station as a means of 'Nepalizing' the region to the benefit of the regiments. The Charter did much to bring the Gurkha regiments fully into the fold of the Indian army, at least geographically, but modern pressures began to alter the balance of the matter during the 20th century: the 3rd Gurkhas were moved from Almora in 1939, and the other two original regiments were shifted at the time of the 1947 partition of India. The original Charter homes of the 4th and 5th Gurkhas were Bakloh and Abbottabad.

Back on the North-East Frontier the British garrison forces were involved during the 1870s and 1880s in a fairly constant series of small-scale campaigns to preserve the peace and permit the growth of British influence. Thus there was a constant drain on the manpower strengths of the regiments involved: rarely did any one campaign cost more than a dozen or so men, but to these had to be added the greater losses suffered from disease, so a small but steady stream of reinforcements was required to keep the battalions up to strength. The 42nd Regiment continued to play a key part in the

Close ties have been forged between the Gurkhas and a number of Scottish regiments as a result of several martial exploits. These are the heliograph-equipped regimental signallers of The Argyll and Sutherland Highlanders, 1894.

With their rifles at the trail, a battalion of Gurkhas marches past the reviewing stand at a parade held in Agra during January 1897.

area, and was slowly joined by other regiments: the arrival of the 2nd Goorkhas has already been mentioned, and other forces were the 43rd and 44th Regiments, which had with the 2nd and 4th Goorkha Regiments played a part in the Bhutan War of 1865–6. There had for some time been a smouldering border dispute between the kingdom of

The Gurkha regiments have always maintained a familial approach to regimental life, resettlement and maintenance of retired Gurkha soldiers being an important duty to each battalion. Frequent reunions were and are held, the one illustrated being at Delhi on 14 September 1907.

The Gurkhas are by origin basically a hill people, and, as such, have proved themselves masterly exponents of warfare in mountainous terrain. This is a party of Gurkha riflemen during the Black Mountain campaign of 1888, the rifles being Lee Metford magazine weapons, which did much for firepower without loss of accuracy compared with that of the earlier Martini-Henry rifles.

Bhutan and the British in India, and in January 1865 the exasperated British decided to send a small expeditionary force into Bhutan to settle the matter on a permanent basis. A garrison was established at Dewangiri, but the Bhutanese caught this small force totally unawares and expelled it from the country. More than slightly piqued by this reverse, the Indian government decided that sterner measures were required, and under General Sir Henry Tombs an expeditionary force was sent into the country. This time no underestimation of the

Bhutanese was permitted, and the expeditionary force compelled the Bhutanese to sue for terms in November, the final treaty being signed in 1866.

Trouble had continued relatively unabated ever since the end of the 1st Burma War, whose conclusion in favour of the British had failed to root out the basic points of dissent. The 2nd Burma War of 1852–3 resulted, and this too was inconclusive: as a result of their military successes the British (in the form of the Honourable East India Company) annexed the southern part of Burma (Pegu province) with the tacit approval of Mindon Min, who overthrew his half-brother Pagan Min as king of Burma. There matters rested uneasily for some 35 years, though the 'peace' was marred by a succession of border squabbles and increasing internal unrest within Burma. In 1878 Mindon Min died, and was succeeded by his son Thibaw Min, a generally inadequate ruler who saw his main chance of

Mountain operations are best supported by specialist artillery, and the Gurkha regiments frequently had their own organic artillery for the task, this being the 42nd Gurkha Gun Team in 1890. Weapons such as these were light and handy enough for mountain operations, but had adequate range and shell power to deal with moderately powerful fortifications.

restoring Burma's fortunes, and of quelling internal unrest, as lying with the promotion of Franco–British rivalry in the thriving teak trade. This was the immediate cause of the 3rd Burma War (1885), though Burmese involvement in Manipur's border problems was also a contributory factor.

The British plan was to send a powerful army force up the Irrawaddy river in a large flotilla of Royal Navy steam ships to take the Burmese capital, Ava. Under the overall command of General H.N.D. Prendergast, the British force numbered some 9000 troops, and included three Gurkha battalions, namely the 3rd (The Kumaon) Goorkha Regiment, the 42nd (Assam) Regiment of Bengal Light Infantry, and the 44th (Sylhet) Regiment of Bengal Light Infantry. The pattern of the campaign was typical: losses were suffered from the Burmese, but greater losses resulted from disease. Nevertheless the British force approached Ava by November 1885, and Thibaw Min capitulated. The formal treaty was signed in 1886, and as part of this the British annexed the rest of Burma. This did not signal the end of hostilities, however, and for the next 10 years the British were heavily involved in a vicious guerrilla war as they pacified the country and brought it under formal British rule. Even with the elimination of the major guerrilla bands, banditry

Throughout Victorian times, the Gurkha regiments functioned with very few British officers, and functioned admirably as a team with native officers of various ranks. Seen here is a group of such native officers belonging to the 1/5th Goorkha Regiment in about 1883.

Top left. The officers of the 4th Gurkha Rifles seen outside their mess in the closing stages of Queen Victoria's reign.

Left. Men of the 5th Goorkha Regiment seen in 1882, shortly before the unit was retitled the 5th Goorkha Regiment, The Hazara Goorkha Battalion.

raged little unabated and it was in an effort to find additional manpower for this task that another Gurkha unit was raised as the Kubo Valley Military Police Battalion. In 1890 this battalion was taken onto the regular establishment as the 1st Regiment of Burma Infantry, in 1891 becoming the 10th (1st Burma Battalion) Regiment of Madras Infantry.

This and comparable campaigns were the standard fare for Indian army regiments after the reorganization that had been made necessary by the Indian mutiny, and by 1886 it was clear that the regular establishment was inadequate to meet all its commitments. It was decided not to increase the number of regiments as such, but rather to expand the existing establishment, and in that year the first five Gurkha regiments were each instructed to raise a second battalion. This proved a relatively simple task, and indeed such was the availability and eagerness of Nepalese hillmen that all five new battalions were raised without delay, the fastest being the 2/2nd Goorkha Rifles being available within a mere three months. It was during this expansion of the Gurkhas that the 42nd Regiment became an all-Gurkha unit, being restyled the 42nd Gurkha Light Infantry.

Before leaving the course of events on the North-East Frontier to see what was happening on the North-West Frontier, thought should be taken for an episode that reflected little credit on the ability of the British to control events in the area, but nonetheless showed the Gurkhas for the excellent fighting men they were. Yet again, the source of the trouble was the border region, this time Manipur where in 1890 the British-recognized rajah was ousted by his younger brother, who refused to accede to British demands that he step down. The British chief commissioner in Assam was J.W.

Quintan, and he decided that punitive action would have to be taken. Accordingly, in March 1891 he set off with a force of some 400 Gurkhas to reinforce the party of 43rd (Goorkha) Regiment acting as escort for the local political officer, F. Grimmond. The whole scheme was misconceived at the political level, and the chances of the plan achieving its primary objective, the capture of the usurper (who was head of the Manipuri army), were remote. For a start, political objections were responsible for the leaving behind of the Gurkhas' mountain guns, whose presence would have helped to redress the considerably numerical inferiority of the Gurkhas. And though intelligence reports spoke of the fact the Manipuris were looking forward to the killing of a major figure (Quintan), nothing was done to ascertain the truth of the report. The force led by Quintan reached the capital, Imphal, without hindrance, but there then followed a disastrous episode in which the British refused to commit themselves to any course of action while the Manipuris played for

Mindful of the chance of booty, Gurkhas search the bodies of the Sikh dead after the Battle of Sobraon on 10 February 1846, when the 1st Sikh War was effectively concluded.

time, and when the moment was ripe invited the senior Gurkha officer, Quintan and Grimmond to a celebration in the palace. The British officers were then seized and killed, leaving the Gurkhas without senior command as they headed back for Assam. Some 200 Gurkhas were left behind in Imphal, and these fought a classic defence of the British residency until they ran out of ammunition. The survivors then fixed bayonets and drew their kukris for a final charge against the large force of Manipuris besieging them. This gallant charge was carried out

One of the great treasures of the 2nd Goorkhas is The Queen's Truncheon, seen here at a parade of the 2/2nd King Edward's Own Gurkha Rifles (The Sirmoor Rifles) on Delhi Day, 14 September 1907 in commemoration of the regiment's hugely distinguished part in the Siege of Delhi in 1857.

with extreme courage, and only some 50 or so Gurkhas survived to fall alive into Manipuri hands.

The humiliation of the event was enormous, and while two Gurkha officers who escaped to Assam were court martialled in secret and then cashiered, a more effective retributive force was raised in the form of three columns that were to take Imphal. Two Gurkha units were involved in this effort,

The escort to the British Resident in Katmandu is pictured in 1863, looking extremely smart and capable.

Gurkhas train on the exercise area at the Abbottabad depot during January 1908. Note the pack mules for the movement of ammunition boxes. The rifleman's weapon was by this time the Rifle No. 1, a weapon whose comparative lightness and short length was well suited to the relative slightness of the average Gurkha's physique.

namely the 42nd (Gurkha) Rifle Regiment and the 1st/2nd Gurkha Rifles. Realizing the impossibility of their position by this time, the Manipuris put up only a token resistance to the British advance, and after the capture of Imphal the British tried and executed the ringleaders of the earlier regime. Yet again, however, battle casualties were far exceeded by losses to disease, of which the two most virulent were cholera and malaria: the 42nd lost 58 officers and men to disease, and the 1/2nd 32 officers and men. In each case the fatalities exceeded 50 per cent of those struck down by disease. It is a telling example of the problems faced by the soldier of the time in such unhealthy regions.

While these constant but generally small-scale operations had been proceeding on the North-East Frontier, more momentous occurrences had been occupying the attentions of the British forces on the North-West Frontier, where the expansive ambitions of Russia were making themselves increasingly felt during the second half of the 19th century. And while the second half of the 19th century on the

Well-ordered camp life has long been a feature of military life, for the Gurkhas as well as for other troops, and this is visible in this illustration of a base camp for the 1892 Black Mountain expedition.

Top left. Men of the 1/5th Gurkha Rifles set up a machine-gun position with the aid of their British officer during one of the many punitive operations undertaken in the period before World War I. This action took place in 1908 as an Indian Army field force swept a dissident area.

Left. The Chitral campaign of 1895 involved long marches through inhospitable country, as indicated by the snow faced by this group of 3rd Goorkha (Rifle) Regiment infantrymen at the foot of the Sowarai Pass.

North-East Frontier was notable for the decreasing need for military activity as the local tribes and peoples became accustomed to the British presence and the general equability of British rule, the same most certainly did not occur on the North-West Frontier, where the British faced if anything an increasing scale of opposition as the century advanced, and where the local tribesmen and peoples steadfastly refused to accept the existence and advantages of British rule over their long-established local traditions.

By the time of the Indian mutiny the British were already established in the Punjab, even if large segments of the Sikh community were still antagonistic, and in the aftermath of the mutiny pushed forward into the hill regions separating India from Afghanistan. Here lived the notably martial Pathan peoples of many tribes, who were accustomed to a way of life that bore no resemblance to what were now arbitrary boundaries between India and Afghanistan. From time immemorial, the Pathans rightly claimed, they had moved with their herds to either side of the hills as the needs for pasture dictated. The British in India were aware of the fact and prepared to accept that such a semi-nomadic existence should continue. But in London the situation appeared intolerable, for the Pathans were seen as tools of the Russians able to destabilize great frontier regions while spying the lie of the land for the Russians who were known to be wooing the Afghans. The authorities in India were thus instructed that the Pathans must be immobilized and the North-West Frontier regions heavily garrisoned to this end and to prevent any Russian incursion into the area through the limited number of passes.

The seeds were thus sown for a period of continuous and increasingly bitter warfare. Yet previously matters had seemed well set for a more stable and amicable future: Afghanistan had supplied the Sikhs with useful support during the 2nd Sikh War, but by the Treaty of Peshawar in 1855 between the British and Dost Mohammed, the king of Afghanistan, the Peshawar region was confirmed as a British annexation in return for British support of the Afghan regime in its successful attempts to regain the Balkh, Kandahar and Herat regions. Though the Indian mutiny offered Dost Mohammed a golden opportunity to strike at the British when they were otherwise overextended and totally vulnerable, he abided by the terms of the treaty, remained neutral and concentrated on filling the power vacuum in Herat left by the withdrawal of the Persians who had laid claim to the region. But though Dost Mohammed gained control of the Herat region in 1863, he died almost immediately afterwards and was succeeded by his son, Sher Ali. Sher Ali enjoyed by no means total loyalty in Afghanistan, and the country was thus soon torn by internal strife as Sher Ali's cousin, Abdur Rahman, sought to gain power. Abdur Rahman enjoyed considerable popular support and was a capable general, so generally prevailed in the armed clashes that shook Afghanistan for the next 16 years. The British were at this time vacillating about exactly what policy they should adopt for the North-West Frontier, so Sher Ali decided that greater benefit would accrue to his cause from a relationship with Russia. Confident in Russian support, Sher Ali became increasingly hostile to the British, who were highly alarmed by the inroads made into the region by the Russian support for Sher Ali.

By 1878 the position was intolerable so far as the British were concerned, and the Viceroy of India, Lord Lytton, decided that Sher Ali had to be taught a military lesson so that he would renounce his Russian relationship. The final straw, so far as Lytton was concerned, was that a Russian envoy had been received with every courtesy in Afghanistan while the British envoy, Sir Neville Chamberlain, had been turned back at the frontier. A substantial force was raised for the Afghan expedition: the Peshawar Valley Field Force, commanded by Lieutenant General Sir Sam Browne, VC; the Kurrum Valley Field Force, commanded by Major General Sir Frederick Roberts, VC; and the Kandahar Field Force commanded by Lieutenant General Donald Stewart. Gurkha units attached to the expeditionary force were the 4th Goorkhas (Peshawar Valley Field Force) and 5th Goorkhas (Kurrum Valley Field Force).

The British plan called for a three-prong advance through the hills into Afghanistan, drawing in and defeating piecemeal any Afghan forces that tried to resist the British advance. First to see action was the Peshawar Valley Field Force, which crossed the frontier on 21 November 1878 at Jamrud and drove

Even when they were not abroad on expeditionary operations, the forces on India's North-West Frontier were in a state of constant readiness against surprise attack. This is Fort Lockhart, garrisoned in 1898 by the 2nd (The Prince of Wales's Own) Gurkha (Rifles) Regiment (The Sirmoor Rifles).

Seen taking his ease at the entrance to his tent is Major General Sir Frederick Roberts, VC, commander of the Kurrum Valley Field Force in the 2nd Afghan War. The guard is provided by the 3rd Sikhs and the 5th Goorkha Regiment.

A contemporary illustration shows a Gurkha skirmish line moving forward from the position of the main body. The Gurkhas proved admirably adept at such operations, a skill that bore rich fruit in the patrol operations of World War II.

into Afghanistan, capturing the major fortress of Ali Masjid on the next day. In its sector the Kurrum Valley Field Force also pushed across the frontier and headed into Afghanistan, and it was this force that decided the initial outcome of the campaign: Sher Ali took to the field with his main force against the Kurrum Valley Field Force, concentrating the Afghan main strength in an excellent position at Peiwar Kotal. Roberts had the measure of the Afghans, however, and whatever the misguided

Though the Battle of the Dargai Heights in the course of the Tirah campaign of 1897 was an extremely costly victory for the Tirah Expeditionary Force, which included six Gurkha battalions, it further consolidated the good relations between the Gurkhas (in the form of the 1/3rd Gurkhas) and The Gordon Highlanders. Marked A and B on the photograph are the two ridges that feature so prominently in accounts of the battle.

political objectives of the 2nd Afghan War, there can be little doubt that in purely military terms the whole affair was considerably better managed than the 1st Afghan War, in which the generals had been old and working in a virtual intelligence vacuum. Like the other senior commanders, Roberts was in his virile 50s, experienced and well provided with intelligence of the Afghans' strength and capabilities. Moreover, Roberts commanded high-grade, experienced troops, and thus felt able to tackle the Peiwar Kotal position with a potentially disastrous outflanking move undertaken at night: leaving his artillery in a frontal position to simulate the activities of the whole field force, Roberts led his infantry onto the Afghans' flank and attacked on 2 December. The Afghans were tactically dismayed by the appearance of the British main strength on their flank, but put up a determined resistance before finally breaking to

flee into the interior. The 5th Goorkhas performed with some distinction, and among them Captain John Cook won the Victoria Cross. Despite the initial severity of the fighting, the British lost only 10 dead and 88 wounded, but the defeat of Sher Ali in this battle had decisive results: Roberts annexed the Kurrum Valley, and while fleeing Sher Ali died before securing any promise of Russian aid. Sher Ali was succeeded by his son, Yakub Khan, who was nominally better disposed towards the British. Thus in May 1879 a treaty was signed between Yakub Khan and the British, whereby in return for an annual subsidy of £60,000 and a promise of British support for Afghanistan in the event of aggression by a third nation, Yakub Khan ceded the Kurrum and Pisheen valleys, permitted the permanent garrisoning of the Khyber Pass by British forces and, most importantly of all so far as Delhi and London were concerned, agreed to the installation of a British Resident in Kabul. Little known to the British, however, it was this last which caused the Afghans the gravest disquiet, for they remained perfectly convinced that the imposition of a Resident meant that inevitable British annexation would follow.

The Resident was to be Sir Louis Cavagnari, and with an escort of 77 Guides he reached Kabul on 24 July 1879. Meanwhile Afghan unrest had continued without respite: Yakub Khan was unpopular as the man who had opened the political gates to the British, and his decision to replace all local army units who had been defeated by the British with fresh troops from the west was politically and militarily unsound. These replacements had no practical experience of British military capabilities, and when offered only one month of their six months back pay immediately rebelled and headed for the

General Sir Robert Low makes an inspection of the Chitral Expeditionary Force somewhere in Chitral during 1895. Three Gurkha regiments were involved in this foray by the Indian Army into the extreme north-west of the country.

Ceremonial played an important morale and training role in the Indian Army, and although the Gurkhas lacked the gorgeous uniforms of many other regiments, their rifle green dress possessed its own attraction, as indicated by this parade of the 1/2nd Gurkha (Rifles) Regiment at Dehra Dun during June 1899.

The Battle of Peiwar Kotal was an Indian army success at the beginning of the 2nd Afghan War in December 1878, the 5th Goorkha Regiment of Roberts's Kurrum Valley Field Force particularly distinguishing itself after a night flanking march to out-manoeuvre and then outfight the Afghans of Sher Ali, who were routed.

An honour guard of four riflemen supports the extra native officer carrying The Queen's Truncheon presented to The Sirmoor Battalion by Queen Victoria in honour of its part in suppressing the Indian Mutiny. The battalion had previously been awarded an honorary third colour for its part in the Siege of Delhi, but with the elevation of the unit to the status of a rifle regiment had lost the right to carry colours. The truncheon was a unique replacement for the third colour.

British residency, where vast sums of money were fondly believed to exist. Thus on 3 September 1879 Cavagnari, his whole escort and party, and all the British in Kabul, were massacred. Yet the Guides sold their lives dearly in the 12-hour action, killing no fewer than 600 Afghans.

Retribution was not long in coming, for the government of India could under no circumstances permit such an event to occur without punishment even if Yakub Khan blamed the massacre on rebellious troops and mob violence. Roberts was ordered to march on Kabul from positions in the Kurrum Valley and from Kandahar, and little time was lost before the British set out with 7500 men and 22 guns of the Kabul Field Force, which included the 5th Goorkhas. Afghan resistance was at first negligible, though a major concentration was taking place at Charasia, where the Afghans assembled

some 8000 men. Again Roberts eschewed the frontal assault, instead concentrating his weight on the Afghans' left flank. This force comprised mainly the 5th Goorkhas and the 92nd Foot, and the battle on 6 October completely defeated the Afghans, allowing Roberts to take Kabul on 12 October without further resistance. Yakub Khan thereupon abdicated, but further military preparations were clearly in hand, and Roberts sensibly decided not to pin his defensive capability on Kabul, but rather on Sherpur to the north of Kabul. Here the Kabul Field Force selected a powerful defensive position that was soon increased in potential by the careful siting of artillery and field fortifications. By this time Roberts' force had been reinforced, and his Gurkha assets were the 2nd, 4th and 5th Gurkhas. On 23 December 1879

Before the advent of radio communication during the earlier part of the present century, tactical signalling was the responsibility of buglers, heliograph operators, flag signallers and runners, all four methods being employed successfully by the Indian army, as this neatly posed group of 2nd Goorkha signallers indicates.

the Afghans, by now whipped up into a near-frenzy of nationalist and religious fervour, fell upon the British position at Sherpur. It is believed that the Afghans numbered some 100,000, but their organization and planning were nonexistent: Roberts let the first fury spend itself on the outer defences, and then broke out right through the besiegers. Using their mobility and cohesion the British forces then fell upon the Afghan flank yet again, completely breaking them. The Afghan mob dispersed, and the British were then able to move into the country for a pacification offensive under the command of Sir Donald Stewart.

But all was not over, for earlier in the campaign Ayub Khan, brother of the discredited Yakub Khan, had declared that he would never submit to the British and in January 1879 seized Herat as a base from which to threaten Kandahar. Ayub Khan now claimed the throne of Afghanistan and marched on Kandahar with some 25,000 dedicated tribesmen. The British commander in Kandahar was Lieutenant General James Primrose, who had a relatively low opinion of the Afghans' capabilities. In his offensive-defensive scheme for the defence of Kandahar, therefore, he sent Brigadier General G.R.S. Burrows with a force of only 2500 men to intercept Ayub Khan's advance at Maiwand, some 50 miles to the north-west of Kandahar. The Battle of Maiwand was a disaster for the British on 27 July 1880: the British and Indian troops attacked the Afghans, who were in a carefully chosen position, but immediately began to run into trouble as the artillery ammunition was expended without any break in the Afghan lines. Ayub Khan had clearly learned from the Afghans' previous reverses (principally at the hand of Roberts) and now launched a decisive counterattack on the British flank. The Indian regiments broke, leaving the sole British regiment to stand in the face of insuperable odds. Burrows was finally able to extricate the remnants of his force after losses of some 800 men, and pulled back to Kandahar, which was immediately invested by the jubilant Afghans.

Men of the 6th Gurkha Rifles illustrated by Major (later Major General) A.C. Lovett in 1910.

Men of the 9th Gurkha Rifles pose for the camera during a roadside halt during a training exercise in 1905.

Word of the position at Kandahar soon reached the resourceful Roberts in Kabul, and a special force was immediately put in hand for a forced march to Kandahar. Key to the relief column's eventual success was the specially formulated supply echelon, designed to keep pace with rapid infantry advances. The advance from Kabul started on 9 August, and the British force made remarkable time across inhospitable terrain and through frequent ambushes to reach Kandahar in only 22 days after covering some 313 miles. The feat of the relief column was the more remarkable as it encountered extremes of temperature and during the last stages of the march was struck by fever, this latter making it necessary to carry some 1000 men rather than leave them to the nonexistent mercies of the Afghans.

Arriving outside Kandahar, Roberts wasted no time on lengthy preparations, but immediately fell upon the force of Ayub Khan, securing total tactical surprise. Yet again Roberts used the flanking movement that had brought him so much success against the Afghans: pinned on their front, the Afghans were unable to provide adequate defence for their artillery, which fell to Roberts' flanking movement. But perhaps the most notable part of the whole battle was the classic bayonet charge of the 92nd (Gordon) Highlanders and 2nd Goorkhas, who were now well established as partners in the brigade commanded by Brigadier General McPherson, an ex-commandant of the 2nd Goorkhas. This partnership had begun during the Battle of Sherpur on 24 December 1879, when the Afghan main body, established on a hilltop, had been assaulted by the 92nd, the 72nd and the Sikhs with two companies of the 2nd Goorkhas in support: the attack had initially been delayed and indeed almost halted by the Afghans' rapid and accurate fire, but the British and Indian forces had eventually stormed the hilltop and forced the Afghans to fall back for fear of encirclement.

In the Battle of Kandahar Colonel Battye, commanding the 2nd Goorkhas, was wounded early in the action, leaving Major White of the 92nd Highlanders to order the charge. The two battalions stormed up the hill that constituted the Afghans' main position, despite the receipt of concentrated rifle fire from the massed defenders. Losses were heavy, especially on the Afghan side, but the two battalions took the hilltop and the two guns sited there in support of the defence: a celebrated painting shows a Gurkha stuffing his cap into the muzzle of one of the guns as an indication that it was a prize of the 2nd Goorkhas, and indeed the gun was later presented to the regiment by the government of India. The Afghans lost more than 1000 casualties in this sector of the Battle of Kandahar, and the besieging force broke and headed for Herat. The lifting of the siege of Kandahar ended military resistance of an organized nature and the British were able to consolidate their position in Afghanistan. A pro-British government was established under Abdur Rahman, and in 1881 the British pulled out of Afghanistan. Yet again the Gurkhas had distinguished themselves, and further close links between Gurkha and British regiments had been forged and tempered in the heat of action.

One of the lessons of the Afghan wars most eagerly devoured by the British was that they should under no circumstances underestimate the military capabilities of the peoples on the North-West Frontier. There had for some time previous to these wars been a feeling that while the frontier tribesman might be a capable and courageous fighter, skilled in the use of his rifle and well able to take full advantage of natural terrain features, he was nevertheless an individual, and that the hill tribes and peoples therefore lacked the organizational ability to produce effective armies of soldiers rather than individual fighters. The Afghan wars dispelled this rather patronizing attitude in a welter of casualties and expense. Yet the lessons had been there for the British to learn some time before the Afghan wars, notably the Umbeyla campaign of 1863. This was an offshoot of the semi-permanent state of military affairs on the North-West Frontier, which had already evolved into a pattern of small-scale raids and counter-raids that kept the British garrison forces on the alert against the Pathan tribesmen.

But with the end of the Indian mutiny, many of the more capable (and more dedicated) of the mutineers had escaped the British net and moved west to link up with these Pathan tribesmen. Thus the basic skills of the hill peoples were combined with the training and fanaticism of the mutineers to produce what became known as the Sitana Fanatics, who had by 1863 become a considerable thorn in the side of the British. It was decided at this stage that the Sitana Fanatics must be destroyed by a properly organized expedition, and the Yusafzai Field Force was raised under Sir Neville Chamberlain with the intention of marching through the Mahaban mountain region to destroy the fanatics' headquarters in a village called Malka. It was anticipated that the approach march to the Mahaban region would present few problems, for though the terrain was difficult, and crossed only by a single pass, the local Bunerwal tribe was hostile to the Sitana Fanatics. But with a lack of forethought all too typical of the British in India, it was deemed unnecessary to keep the Bunerwalis informed of British intentions. Thus the Sitana Fanatics were able to persuade the Bunerwalis that the British were not after the Fanatics alone, but also intended to annex the Bunerwalis' territory. This persuaded the Buner-

The pipes and drums of the 2/1st Gurkha (Rifle) Regiment practise on a parade ground typical of that found at Gurkha depots in the hills of northern India. It is 1897.

The Battle of Peiwar Kotal at the beginning of the 2nd Afghan War involved some extremely difficult and potentially disastrous nocturnal manoeuvres by the forces under Major General Roberts, though the eventual rout of the Afghans fully justified the risks. Here men of the 5th Gurkhas storm into the Afghans' gun line with Scots' support.

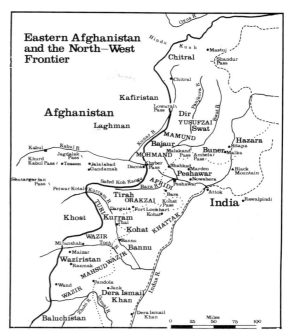

walis to throw in their lot with the Fanatics, and when the Yusafzai Field Force began to enter the Swat valley on 20 October 1863 it began to meet increasing Bunerwali resistance, and within a few days the whole area was up in arms against the British, whose forces included the 4th Goorkhas.

The British were soon in a parlous position, unable to advance into the Swat valley proper, and with their lines of communication wholly vulnerable to a Bunerwali raid. In effect the Yusafzai Field Force was trapped, its position being a small plateau whose flanks were protected by pickets on two peaks. The more important of these was known as the Crag, and it was the scene of much fighting as it was taken and retaken three times. On 13 November, for example, the Crag was taken from the British and retaken only on the third attempt and after the British had suffered heavy casualties. Only one week later the Crag was again lost, and this time recaptured in a counterattack by the 4th Goorkhas and the 71st Highland Light Infantry under the personal command of Chamberlain, who was wounded for the ninth time as part of the British total of 27 dead and 110 wounded. The British managed to hold on until the arrival of reinforcements during December, when the advance was resumed. The Bunerwalis fell back before this strengthened push, but finally made a stand in the Chalma valley and in front of the village of Umbeyla, where they were decisively beaten. The Bunerwalis realized the futility of further resistance and so sued for peace, which was readily granted on the condition that they undertake the dispersion of the Sitana Fanatics under British supervision.

The Umbeyla campaign was a small affair, and of little moment in the history of India and the world.

But the lessons were there for the British to learn. The two most important lessons were clear: that the local tribesmen could be and were formidable opponents when forced into a corner in their own territory, circumstances helping them to overcome their natural reluctance to co-operate; and that it was all too easy (and all too fatal) to ignore the sensibilities of the hill tribesmen by failing to inform them of British intentions. The area was rife with suspicion of everyone's motives, yet a simple piece of local communication could have removed the Bunerwali threat even before it appeared, and so have saved the army in India not inconsiderable casualties and additional expense.

After the Afghan wars the lessons were truly appreciated, and local reforms were instituted to remove the worst aspect of British operations on the North-West Frontier. Local intelligence operations were much expanded and improved so that the intentions and dispositions of the potential hostiles could better be appreciated; training of the garrison forces in hill warfare was intensified; additional British officers were drafted into the Indian and Gurkha regiments; and though ceremonial and social matters were little scaled down in actual quantity, a greater emphasis was placed on the garrison regiments' ability to act quickly and effect-

The hall of the officers' mess at the depot of the 2nd Gurkha Rifles in the early years of the present century bears eloquent testimony to the style in which the British officers lived and to the primary interests of the officers when not on duty. Yet, despite this very British approach to personal comfort and communal living, the officers of the Gurkha regiments then as now rejoiced in a very close 'family' relationship with their men.

ively through the instigation of regular manoeuvres and the maintenance of equipment and supplies at a moment's notice to march. All these made the British and Indian forces on the North-West Frontier highly capable in their specific tasks, which was just as well as the scale and intensity of local opposition increased throughout the last quarter of the nineteenth century.

The period is also notable for the first overseas postings of Gurkha regiments. Appropriately enough, the first Gurkha unit to serve overseas was the 1st Goorkha Regiment (Light Infantry), which shipped out to the Malay States in 1875 after the

murder of the British Resident. Order was restored relatively swiftly, but the regiment was soon involved in the local round of small-scale operations against pirates, local dissidents and the like.

The second Gurkha unit to serve overseas was the 2nd Goorkha Regiment, which in 1878 was posted to the island of Malta to bolster the strategic garrison during the Russo–Turkish War of 1877–8. This provides yet further proof of the constant worry posed throughout the period to the British government by the military ambitions (real and imagined) of an expansionist Russian state. The 2nd Goorkhas returned to India just in time for the main part of the 2nd Afghan War, whose opening stages the regiment missed before catching up with Roberts' forces in time for the Battle of Sherpur.

Such was the nature of events on the North-West Frontier that not many years passed without the need for British punitive measures, and the Gurkhas were at times heavily involved in such expeditions. The policy of the British was on the whole fairly lenient: small raids and the like were generally tolerated, but should they continue unabated or begin to develop into larger affairs, then it was time to deal with the dissidents with a punitive expedition to confiscate weapons and impose monetary sanctions, or alternatively to burn crops and a few small villages as an indication of the Indian government's displeasure. Occasionally, however, there were more serious disturbances directed not so much against the British but rather against neighbours with whom long-standing grievances could almost invariably be found.

A fine example of this last type of conflict can be found in the Chitral campaign, which stemmed from the long-term ambitions towards this small state entertained by the neighbouring state of Jandol, which had a long history of anti-British sentiment. Thus the death of the ruler of Chitral in 1892 signalled a new round in this dispute: waiting for the normally internecine hereditary disputes to weaken the potential opposition, Umra Khan of Jandol then moved his forces into the country against negligible opposition. The British saw the possibility of the dispute flaring up into an altogether more dangerous struggle in this volatile region, and ordered that the Jandoli forces should leave the country. Umra Khan refused, and a small punitive force was sent into Chitral under Sir George Robertson, who also deposed the Chitrali ruler and substituted his younger brother. The effect was a semi-concerted front against the British, who were besieged in Chitral town. The inevitable relief column was immediately assembled, these forces including the second battalions of the 2nd, 4th and 5th Gurkhas. However, by the time that this major relief column reached Chitral the besieged garrison had already been relieved by a column that had fought its way through from Gilgit. To prevent a resurgence of this problem, a fort was built at Malakand in 1897, and this was garrisoned well into the 1930s by men of the 4th Gurkhas.

The Chitral affair had, as a result of swift action by the British, not come to anything dangerous. However, in 1897 an altogether more dangerous situation flared up in various parts of the North-West Frontier as a result of high-running feelings amongst Afridi and Waziri tribesmen. In an effort to quell anti-British activities, the usual retaliatory methods were tried, but in this instance met with determined opposition, particularly from the Waziris. The opening stages of what was to become a serious problem reached a peak with a Waziri attack on a political officer and his escort in the Tochi valley, and with an attack on Malakand by Swati and Mohmand tribesmen. Then the Afridis and Orakzaies joined the dissidents, and by August 1897 the rebels were in control of the Khyber Pass. The government clearly had to act, and to act quickly if the spread of dissension were to be contained.

A considerable expeditionary force was raised, and this included several Gurkha battalions: with the 1st Division of the Tirah Expeditionary Force were the 2/1st Gurkhas and the 2/4th Gurkhas, with the Kurrum Column was the 1/5th Gurkhas, with the Peshawar Column was the 9th Gurkhas, and with the line of communications was the 2/2nd Gurkhas. The strategic plan, such as it was, for this Tirah campaign was straightforwardly simple: the British would push into the hinterland of the tribal areas confiscating weapons, destroying dissident bands, and burning crops and villages where resistance was met. In the early stages, however, most of the resistance came from the heat, which was high even for the Kohat region. The British suffered a number of heatstroke casualties, and progress was further slowed by the tribesmen's clever tactics of hitting and running, which caused the British further losses in time as well as in men, but offered little chance for counterattack by the better trained though slower British and Indian troops.

So far as the Gurkhas were concerned, the high spot of the campaign was the Battle of Dargai Ridge on 18 October 1897. Dargai village was a centre of the Afridi resistance, perched on a rocky outcrop overlooked in turn by the ridge above it. In a direct assault on 18 October, the 3rd Gurkhas and the King's Own Scottish Borderers cleared the Dargai Ridge, so giving the British a commanding position in the area. However, as night fell the Gurkhas and KOSBs were pulled back from the ridge to help consolidate a British position in the village, allowing the Afridis to reoccupy the ridge. This fact was discovered at dawn, and rather than assault the position directly once more, the British decided to bring up their artillery. The delay was nearly fatal, for during the day and the following night the

Afridis set about the construction of an interlocking field of *sangars* (one-man revetments built of loose stone). Thus by the time that the British were ready to resume the attack on 20 October, it was soon appreciated that there were upwards of 12,000 Afridis in carefully chosen and well protected positions on the heights overlooking the entire British position and forming-up area. Tactical surprise was impossible in the circumstances, and the British force of four battalions was seen readying itself: the 2nd Gurkhas in the lead with support from the Dorsets, with the 92nd and 95th in reserve. The advance started at 10.00, the British being agreeably surprised by the lack of Afridi response. But what the British command did not appreciate, having failed signally to undertake any real reconnaissance of the area, was that the Afridis were emplaced

behind an open saddle some 300 yards in width, across which the British would have to advance without any cover against the massed fire of the Afridi rifles. Colonel Eaton Travers of the 2nd Goorkhas was in local command, and he ordered the final rush by the Goorkhas and Dorsets to their left. The Gurkhas and British stormed over the lip of the saddle into full view of the Afridis, who with commendable restraint had awaited this moment. Immediately a withering fire was opened on the advance, and some 60 Gurkhas fell within seconds. As an eye witness later recorded 'the whole line of sangars burst into smoke and flame and a torrent of bullets from front, right and left, tore through the ranks; men literally fell in heaps and the stony slope was strewed with killed and wounded . . .'

Further advance was clearly impossible, and the survivors of the Gurkhas and Dorsets took shelter under the edge of the lip they had just crossed. By this time the British artillery was available, but could not contribute at all effectively because of the lie of

The dining room of the officers' mess of the 2nd Gurkha Rifles at Dehra Dun in 1905 shows the style in which the British officers lived. At each end of the mantelpiece are trumpets captured in the Tibetan expedition of 1903.

the ground. Thus it was left for the infantry to try again, this time with the Gordons and the 3rd Sikhs in the lead with the Gurkhas in support. Supported by the artillery, the attack was resumed by this augmented infantry force, and the Afridis chose this time to melt away, leaving the British in command of the heights. Thus the victory finally went to the British, but only at the cost of considerable casualties right at the beginning of the campaign, while the Afridis melted away with hardly a man injured, jubilant that in the right circumstances they were more than a match for the British.

Thereafter the British columns were able to press ever deeper into the tribal lands, never again finding a sizable force in opposition, but having the whole time to guard against ambushes and snipers, the harassment of parties on the force's lines of communication, and the wiping out of patrols and pickets. October and November 1897 marked the beginning of the end for the dissident tribesmen, and by the start of 1898 the British were within sight of their goals: the passes were again in British hands, and large numbers of tribesmen had opted to pay fines of money or rifles to avoid the continued presence of the British within their lands. Yet again, therefore, the British were able to capitalize on the discipline and endurance of their troops to outlast the tribesmen, who lacked the stomach for prolonged campaigns against cohesive forces.

Meanwhile great changes were being planned for the Indian army, and these materially affected the nature and status of the Gurkha regiments, which had increased to a total of 10 by 1891. The original five regiments were now known as the 1st to 5th Gurkha Regiments, all of them rifle regiments. The other five were the 9th (Gurkha Rifles) Regiment of Bengal Infantry, the 42nd (Gurkha Rifles) Regiment of Bengal Infantry, the 43rd (Gurkha Rifles) Regiment of Bengal Infantry, the 44th (Gurkha Rifles) Regiment of Bengal Infantry, and the 10th Regiment (1st Burma Battalion) of Madras Infantry. It was now decided that all the Gurkha regiments should be listed on a common basis, and logic would have dictated that the latter five regiments should be allocated the numberings 6th to 10th Regiments according to their seniority. But this was not to be, for the logic of the Indian army was not the same as the logic of others, and these modifications to the

The Kilmarnock cap, often known as the pillbox cap, has been associated with Gurkha regiments for some time as indicated by this photograph of Gurkhas with a wheeled (but by no means manoeuvrable) Maxim machine-gun complete with defensive shield for use in semi-permanent positions.

Gurkhas' nomenclature were also caught up in the basic restructuring of the Indian army undertaken in 1901. It had been clear for some time that the old organization of the Indian army, based on the organization of the armies of the three Honourable East India Company presidencies (Bengal, Madras and Bombay), was hopelessly out of date in a time of rapidly evolving military situations and tactics. In 1901, therefore, the Indian army was remodelled on a more rational basis reflecting the new tactics, with all the regiments placed on a common list. The original five regiments of Gurkhas thus became the 1st to 5th Gurkha Rifles, and the next five places were occupied by the newer regiments, though not in the order of their seniority as would have seened sensible. Thus the senior and junior regiments (namely the 9th Bengal and 10th Madras) became the 9th and 10th Gurkha Rifles respectively, while the intervening places were occupied in 1903 by the 42nd, 43rd and 44th Regiments as the 6th, 7th and

8th Gurkha Rifles respectively. Thus was formed the Brigade of Gurkhas, which lasted in that basic form until the partition of 1947 forced a complete reorganization upon this long-established force.

It is worth noting, however, that this 1903 organization was reached only through a number of interim steps. In 1902, for example, another Gurkha battalion had been raised in Burma; this was originally designated the 8th Gurkha Rifles and at first contained men from the 10th Gurkha Rifles and other Gurkhas serving in the civil forces in Burma. But when the 44th Regiment became the 8th Gurkha Rifles in 1903, the 1902 regiment became the 2nd Battalion of the 10th Gurkha Rifles. Further change followed in 1907: the 7th and 8th Gurkha Rifles (formerly the 43rd and 44th Regiments) were amalgamated as the 1st and 2nd Battalions of the 8th Gurkha Rifles, leaving the name 7th Gurkha Rifles free for the 2nd Battalion of the 10th Gurkha Rifles. By 1908 each of the 10 regiments had a second battalion, an arrangement made possible by a revised agreement with the government of Nepal, which sanctioned a level of recruitment to maintain 20 battalions of Gurkhas on the strength of the Indian army. By this time it had become policy for the regiments to recruit exclusively from the hill tribes, and the Terai Gurkhas slowly disappeared from British service. The increasingly special niche of the Gurkhas within the Indian establishment was also recognized by the awarding of special honorifics: thus in 1906 the 1st Gurkha Rifles (The Malaun Regiment) became the 1st Prince of Wales Own Gurkha Rifles, and in 1910 the 1st King George's Own Gurkha Rifles; in 1906 the 2nd (The Prince of Wales's Own) Gurkha Rifles (The Sirmoor Rifles) became the 2nd King Edward's Own Gurkha Rifles (The Sirmoor Rifles); and in 1907 the 3rd Gurkha Rifles became the 3rd The Queen's Own Gurkha Rifles and in 1908 the 3rd Queen Alexandra's Own Gurkha Rifles.

While these changes were being planned and implemented, the Gurkhas were again involved in the almost unending round of border disputes and squabbles. The 2nd Gurkhas were embroiled in a flare-up in Waziristan during 1901 and 1902 that was settled without much bloodshed but was otherwise notable for the introduction of the 'pillbox' hat that is now considered to be traditional Gurkha head-gear. This proved its suitability in the Waziristan campaign and was thus adopted for all the Gurkha regiments. The other major operation to involve Gurkha troops during this period was the expedition taken into Tibet by Colonel Francis Younghusband in 1903. The threat of Russian expansion towards the Indian Ocean was still very real to the British, particularly the authorities in India, and at the turn of the century serious fears were entertained about the growth of Russian influence in Tibet with the acquiescence of the Dalai Lama. A small diplomatic mission was despatched to negotiate with the Dalai Lama, who refused to have anything to do with the mission, which established itself at Khamba Jone just inside the Tibetan frontier to await further developments by the Tibetans and Chinese.

Matters were brought to a head in the autumn of 1903 by the arrest in Sikkim (part of India) of two 'spies' by the Tibetans. So flagrant a disregard for Indian sovereignty could not be allowed to pass without counteraction (despite the equally provocative installation of the diplomatic mission on Tibetan soil!), so a small but well-equipped expeditionary force was sent into Tibet, its task being to press no farther than Gyantse, some 100 miles short of the Tibetan capital, Lhasa. Included in this force were the 8th Gurkha Rifles.

The British force had a desperate time of it in the abysmal cold and extremely high winds as it crossed into Tibet through the Jelap La pass in the Himalayas. Marching at an altitude of some 17,000 ft, the British troops encountered problems hitherto unimagined, including the freezing of the oil in their weapons and the death of many beasts of burden. No resistance was encountered at first, but a body of some 2000 Tibetan troops was finally encountered outside the village of Guru on 31 March 1904. Neither side appeared willing to take the initiative, and Younghusband ordered his men to disarm the Tibetans. Some Tibetans had been deprived of their weapons when their commander finally gave the order to fire, and a bitter but short battle followed: raked by the fire of two machine-guns, the Tibetans were slaughtered in large numbers: some 900 Tibetan dead were counted, while the British casualties amounted to a mere six wounded. Younghusband then pushed forward to Gyantse, which was reached without further incident. The British force then settled down to await developments, hopefully in the form of emissaries from the Dalai Lama so that negotiations could be started.

What did appear, however, was another large Tibetan force, and on 6 July 1904 there took place the Battle of Gyantse. The Tibetans fought with enormous courage, but the British possessed the advantages of discipline and firepower, so prevailing at the cost of many Tibetan dead. During this battle Lieutenant J.D. Grant of the 8th Gurkhas won a Victoria Cross: after falling from a cliff his men were trying to scale, he returned to the fray and so bolstered the enthusiasm of his men that the Tibetan position was overrun. There was nothing left between the British and Lhasa, and Younghusband was thus instructed to proceed with extreme caution to the Tibetan capital, which was reached on 2 August. Again the British settled down to wait, and finally the Dalai Lama decided to bargain: no trace of Russian influence was ever detected, but the British were able to secure advantageous trading rights with the Tibetans. In purely political terms the whole exercise had been futile, but it provided the Gurkhas with another chance to enhance their steadily growing reputation.

Together with other units of the Indian army, the Gurkhas found other small moments of action in the period up to the beginning of World War I, but the importance of this period was in the consolidation of the regiments under their new guises, and the development of the battalions as cohesive fighting entities skilled in the modern tactics that were evolving as a result of British experience in the Boer War coupled with the needs of modern weapons whose efficiency had been proved beyond all doubt by the dreadful losses suffered by the Russian forces in the Russo–Japanese War. The world was moving steadily towards a huge conflict, and the Gurkhas were fully ready to play their part in this climactic event. They had gained invaluable experience in the incessant border campaigns of the North-West and North-East Frontiers, and had proved themselves courageous and capable individual soldiers: now they would face a sterner test in the altogether different conditions of World War I.

British and Gurkha officers of the 1/1st Gurkhas gather outside the battalion headquarters on the northern sector of the Western Front in August 1915.

WORLD WAR I

With the exception of a brief tour in Malta during 1875, the Gurkhas had up to 1914 remained firmly within the orbit of the Indian army's responsibilities for service on the Indian subcontinent and ancillary areas such as Burma and Malaya. World War I was to change all that, not only for the Gurkhas but also for the entire Indian army, which was rapidly swept up into the UK's dire war against Germany and her allies in Europe and on several other fronts. This increased demand for troops from the Indian establishment (then as now an all-volunteer organization) was met readily and with considerable skill. The Gurkhas, for example, swelled in numbers considerably as all but the 4th and 10th Gurkha Rifles raised a third battalion, and a new 11th Gurkha Rifles of four battalions was raised in 1918, making an overall total of 32 Gurkha battalions. Moreover, it should be noted, the defence needs of the Indian empire were still considerable, but Gurkhas were freed for overseas service by the willing loan of nine battalions from the Nepalese establishment for garrison and security duties in India. Yet again, this small kingdom played a small but highly significant part in the well-being of the Indian empire.

Yet all this was in the future when the Indian army began to prepare itself for major war in August 1914. The trouble was that for all its combat experience, the Indian army was little prepared, trained or equipped for a major war: operational experience on the North-East and North-West Frontiers was common, but the Indian soldiers little realized how inadequate such small-scale experience against opposition lacking machine-guns, artillery and field fortification capability would be in the type of conditions into which the Indian soldiers would presently be hurled on a variety of fronts. As far as the Gurkhas were concerned, in recent years only a relatively small number of battalions had experienced any type of combat, and of these undoubtedly the best-prepared was the 1/2nd Gurkha Rifles, which had performed with conspicuous success in several North-West Frontier operations, as noted above. Though some of the regiments, notably the 7th and 10th Gurkha Rifles, had yet to prove themselves in sustained combat, the Gurkhas were generally satisfied that they were capable soldiers, skilled in the use of rifle and kukri knife, fit, well disciplined and admirably suited to the rigours of operations in extremes of heat and cold. But what no one at this stage realized was that World War I was not to be fought as a slightly more advanced version of the Franco–Prussian War of 1870: though few had bothered to analyse its implications, the Russo–Japanese War of 1904–5 had presaged a total transformation of modern warfare, with manoeuvre distinctly subordinate to the overwhelming capabilities of three basically defensive factors, namely the machine-gun, barbed wire and relatively immobile heavy artillery. And in the European context, the Indians and Gurkhas were to be faced with a type of weather they had not previously encountered, namely the combination of moderate cold with considerable rainfall to produce the glutinous fields of heavy mud in which much of World War I was fought, especially on the Western Front. Moreover, the tactics that had worked for small-scale operations against lightly armed hill tribesmen were soon proved woefully deficient in the massive operations carried out on the plains of France.

It is to the undying credit of the Gurkhas that they acclimatized themselves to this wholly atypical environment and then prospered in it, at least in the military field. And the problems faced by the battalions from India were enormous. Quite apart from a geographical and cultural context that was completely alien, the men of the Indian army had to face a gamut of military difficulties: their uniforms were not in the slightest suited to the temperatures and conditions of the Western Front; they lacked items soon regarded as essential, such as grenades and mortars; they had no experience with heavy artillery, aircraft and the like; they had wholly inadequate reserves (usually 10 per cent. when they landed at Marseilles, at a time when single actions might erode battalion numbers by up to 50 per cent and when reinforcements had to be shipped in from India); food and language were enormous problems; and the battalions had inadequate numbers of British officers, usually only 12. This last was particularly important, for the Gurkha battalions' special relationship between officers and men was based on a mutual understanding and trust developed over a period of years.

Many battalions lost most if not all of their original officers in a few months, leaving culture-

Looking somewhat incongruous with their bagpipes, the pipers of the 2/3rd Gurkhas perk up their battalion and some locals in an area just behind the lines in France during early 1915.

shocked battalions with replacements who could not and did not really understand their men and their ways, and who often had only the sketchiest command of the language. Despite these difficulties, however, the men of the Indian army were of vital importance to the Allied cause, the more so because the British 'new army' of volunteers would not become available until the middle of 1915 at the earliest. Thus in 1914 the Indian Corps of two divisions held about one-third of the British sector on the Western Front, this sector constituting about one-tenth of the whole Allied line. The corps was sent a message from the King Emperor in London, and this message clearly reflected the hand of one with considerable experience of the Indian soldier, perhaps Lord Roberts. Among its many noble but apposite sentiments are several rightly designed to

appeal to the best aspects of the Indian soldier: '. . . You will be the first Indian soldiers of the King Emperor who will have the honour of showing in Europe that the sons of India have lost none of their ancient martial instincts . . . In battle you will remember that your religions enjoin on you that to give your life doing your duty is your highest reward . . . You will fight for the King Emperor and your faith, so that history will record the doings of India's sons and your children will proudly tell of the deeds of their fathers . . .'

Nicely calculated the message might have been, but it was just the sort of thing that the Indians and Gurkhas wanted, for its import accurately reflected their loyalties, their religions and their cultural backgrounds. And it was these factors, combining with British leadership and training, that made the Indian and Gurkha soldiers rise above the physical handicaps of the Western Front to emerge as some of the outstanding soldiers of World War I, fully the equal of the best fielded by the British and other Allies. Evidence of this capability can be better attested nowhere more tellingly than in a letter from a German soldier with first-hand experience of warfare against men of the Indian army: 'At first we spoke with contempt of the Indians. Today we learned to look on them in a different light – the Devil knows what the English had put into those fellows ... With a fearful shouting thousands of those brown forms rushed upon us ... At 100 metres we opened a destructive fire which mowed down hundreds but in spite of that the others advanced ... In no time they were in our trenches and truly those brown enemies were not to be despised. With butts, bayonets, swords and daggers we fought each other and we had bitter hard work.' The why and where of this action is irrelevant: it displays the transformation of German contempt into respect, it reveals the nature of trench warfare on the Western Front, and it reveals the great courage and determination of the men of the Indian army.

It is impossible to detail all the involvement of the Gurkha battalions in World War I within a book of small compass, so their tribulations, successes and widespread deployment are best recorded in a series of vignettes set against a brief exposition of the regiments' general deployments. The 1st Gurkha Rifles were in France and Flanders during 1914 and 1915, but with the arrival of fresh British forces during 1915 it was decided that all Indian army infantry would be better deployed to areas in which the climate was more suitable for them, and by the end of the year all Indian infantry had been shifted to hotter climes. Thus the 1st Gurkha Rifles found themselves in Mesopotamia from 1916 to 1918, with battalions also in Palestine in 1917 and 1918. The 2nd Gurkha Rifles sent one battalion to France initially, and a second battalion was then despatched to Mesopotamia, eventually moving into northern Persia after the Russian revolution as part of the British force sent into the area to prevent the spread of dissension into an area vital to the UK's continued supplies of oil. The 3rd Gurkha Rifles sent one battalion to France in 1914 and 1915, and was also heavily involved in the Middle East: while the regiment's main strength was concentrated in Palestine for most of the war, a sizable detachment was allocated to the Arab forces fighting the Turks in Arabia under the leadership of Colonel T.E.

Lawrence; these Gurkhas became mounted infantry, though the mounts in this instance were camels. The 4th Gurkha Rifles was another regiment represented in France during 1914 and 1915, and thereafter served in the eastern Mediterranean and the Middle East, playing a notable part in the disastrous Gallipoli landings and the defence of Egypt before switching its main effort to Mesopotamia. Another regiment heavily involved at Gallipoli was the 5th Gurkha Rifles, which again followed a typical pattern with further involvement in Egypt and in Mesopotamia; it is worth noting that the last men off Gallipoli when the peninsula was finally abandoned in 1915 were men of the 5th Gurkhas. The 6th Gurkha Rifles followed a course comparable with that of the 5th Gurkhas, involving service in Gallipoli, Egypt and Mesopotamia, but culminating with the push into northern Persia during 1918, right to the shores of the great Caspian Sea. The 7th Gurkha Rifles were involved exclusively in the Middle East, largely Palestine and the Mesopotamian theatre. The 8th Gurkha Rifles stretched their net further, for a battalion of this regiment served in France during 1914 and 1915 before the regiment started to play the typical Gurkha role in the Middle Eastern areas of Egypt, Palestine and Mesopotamia. The 9th Gurkha Rifles were also involved in the early stages of World War I in France, but thereafter played a prominent part in the events in Mesopotamia. And finally, the 10th Gurkha Rifles were active in Gallipoli, Egypt and Mesopotamia.

Such a summary can only sketch most lightly the details of the Gurkhas' deployments in World War I: the four major areas in which the Nepalese hillmen served in largest numbers were France, largely as an interim measure while the fresh volunteers of Lord Kitchener's 'new army' were being raised; Gallipoli, which had tactical similarities with the North-West Frontier but on an altogether more concentrated and high-powered level; Egypt and Palestine, where the task was first to protect Egypt from any Turkish incursion across the Suez Canal and then drive forward across the Sinai and north into Palestine; and Mesopotamia, the land centred on the Tigris and Euphrates rivers, constituting a threat to British oil supplies and also a primary area of strategic and religious importance to the Turks.

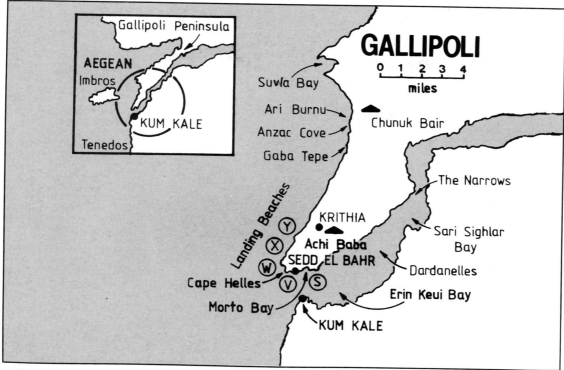

One of the first Gurkha battalions to reach France was the 2/2nd Gurkha Rifles, which disembarked at Marseillès on 15 October 1914 as part of the Dehra Dun Brigade of the Meerut Division. The battalion had been readied for Europe in record time, and in the process had taken up some 150 men of the 1st Battalion. Also in the division was the 2/3rd Gurkha Rifles, brigaded with Garhwalis and the 2nd Leicesters in the Garhwal Brigade. These two Gurkha battalions were soon in the thick of the fighting, each of them winning battle honours at La Bassée, Festubert, Givenchy, Neuve Chapelle and Aubers. At Neuve Chapelle, the 2/3rd Gurkha Rifles were the first British unit into the devastated village, where the advance was temporarily stalled by a concentration of German fire from a relatively undamaged house. On his own initiative, Rifleman Gane Gurung moved into this house without support, emerging a few minutes later with eight captive Germans. It has unfortunately not been recorded how Gane Gurung secured the surrender of the German squad, but his emergence with eight vastly larger charges was greeted with enormous enthusiasm by the men of the Rifle Brigade who had just entered Neuve Chapelle.

It was a man from the same battalion who secured the only Gurkha VC of the French campaign in World War I, though this was the fifth and last awarded to the Indian Corps. The incident occurred during the Battle of Loos during September 1915 as the Indian infantry were already being pulled out of France. During the Battle of Loos the 2/3rd Gurkhas found that the portion of the front allocated to their advance had been little damaged by the preceding artillery barrage: the wire remained intact, and so too did the German machine-gun positions that covered the wire with enfilading fire. The battalion suffered dire losses, but one group of Gurkhas finally managed to penetrate the wire before being killed. However, the attack was completely stalled, with British casualties scattered all over the battlefield. Although himself wounded, Rifleman Kulbir Thapa inexplicably pushed forward through the wire and past the German first trench line, here finding a wounded man of the Leicesters. Kulbir Thapa overrode the Englishman's objections and remained with him throughout the day and the following night, which

*Such were the manpower difficulties faced by the British in
1914 and 1915 that many units of the Indian Army were
drafted into France as a stop-gap measure until British
volunteer units were ready for combat. Battalions such as
this Gurkha unit were unsuited to the cold and damp of the
Western Front and suffered accordingly, though they
performed sterling service until pulled out to warmer climes.*

was marked by the formation of a heavy mist. This
lasted into the second day, allowing Kulbir Thapa to
carry the wounded Englishman back across the
German trench and through the wire to comparative
safety in a shell hole; Kulbir Thapa then made two
trips into the German wire entanglements to find
wounded Gurkhas, and then carried the Englishman
back into the British lines despite the fact that the
mist had lifted. It was a magnificent example of
selfless courage, and fully deserved the award of a
Victoria Cross.

These examples of individual courage reflect well
on the Gurkhas, but also impressive was the steadfast courage of whole units. A classic example of this
can be found in the first major action on the Western
Front endured by the Gurkhas, in this instance the
2/2nd Gurkha Rifles close to the village of Neuve
Chapelle in November 1914. The Gurkhas had

previously seen a limited amount of relatively small-
scale action, but at Neuve Chapelle they encountered for the first time one of World War I's
hallmarks, an intensive artillery bombardment and
co-ordinated infantry assault. The battalion had
moved into the area only three days previously, and
found themselves at the tip of a small salient to one
side of Neuve Chapelle, which was occupied by the
Germans. Immediately the Gurkhas instituted a
programme to develop fixed defences, but these
were uncompleted by the time the Germans un-
leashed their artillery bombardment. Gurkha
casualties were severe, and without an adequate
network of defences in depth, there was every
possibility that the Germans would drive straight
through the battalion, which was by now thoroughly
disorganized. The situation was saved by the
battalion's British officers, who rallied parties of
Gurkha riflemen wherever they could be found and
counterattacked the advancing Germans. All the
officers in the front line were killed during the initial
bombardment or while leading counterattacks, but
their efforts dulled the edge of the German advance,
provided pivots on which a cohesive defence could
begin to form, and encouraged Gurkha officers to

rally the shaken defence on their own initiative. During this episode the battalion lost 38 dead including seven British officers, but began to find itself as an effective fighting unit in a new type of warfare. The Gurkha position was held, and by the end of the day other units had been rushed up to plug the gaps in the line as the battalion was pulled back to regroup and digest more fully the implications of the day.

That the implications had been grasped was indicated on 20 September, when the 2/2nd Gurkhas Rifles' position at La Qinque Rue was blown apart by a German mine: one company was virtually destroyed, but the flanking companies held their ground and thus prevented the Germans from exploiting their possibilities. The battle raged for 48 hours before the Gurkhas handed over an intact position to their relief battalion. Losses were indeed high: 152 officers and men who could not readily be replaced, and who had all the advantages of combat experience on the Western Front.

New drafts were received from India by the Gurkha battalions in France, and these were slowly assimilated into their new units: the process was difficult as the training of the new drafts was not up to the years of experience brought to France by the original battalions, and dead officers could not be replaced instantly by men of comparable capabilities. Nevertheless morale was good and combat capability more than adequate, permitting the Gurkhas to continue in a primary role during the increasingly savage battles of 1915, notably Neuve Chapelle, Aubers Ridge and Loos.

By the end of November 1915 all the Gurkha battalions had been pulled out of the line in France. Some degree of perspective is give to their role by the performance of the 2/2nd Gurkhas, who were withdrawn exactly one year after their first taste of

NCOs of the 2/3rd Gurkhas pose for the camera in front of one of their farmhouse billets in Flanders during August 1915. Though they performed creditably on the Western Front, the Gurkhas were physically unsuited to the conditions of this region.

combat against the Germans: in that year the battalion had suffered 177 dead, and another 825 or more men had been wounded, indicating one-year battalion casualties of over 100 per cent. Despite this fact, recruitment in east and west Nepal remained good, and the battalions had little difficulty in finding numbers of men, even if these lacked the experience of their forebears. In the forcing ground of World War I, however, experience was a commodity that could easily be obtained, even if the expense was often appallingly high.

To the Gurkhas, France was a wholly alien environment that could do little in the long term but blunt the capabilities of hillmen from a drier clime. This fact was readily appreciated by the British authorities, who were also concerned with the logistical effort required to maintain and reinforce Indian and Gurkha troops so far from their home bases. Expediency thus combined with sense to dictate the Indians' and Gurkhas' redeployment to a more accustomed clime; happily for the parties concerned, there were two such areas in the form of Egypt and Mesopotamia, which were also considerably closer to India than was the French battlefield.

Thus the Middle East soon saw the presence of Gurkha battalions, three which saw early service in Egypt being the 2/10th, 1/6th and 2/7th Gurkha Rifles. The 2/10th Gurkha Rifles was soon engaged in the defeat of the Turks' first attempt to seize the Suez Canal, a vital artery in the British war effort. The Turks expressed the uttermost disdain for the British imperial troops in Egypt, especially the Australians, New Zealanders and Indian army units, but had rapid cause to modify this prejudice as their first attack across the canal on 3 February 1915 was handsomely defeated with heavy Turkish casualties. Here it was the Allies who made effective use of the machine-gun, and naval gunfire also played a decisive part. Another Gurkha battalion, the 1/6th Gurkha Rifles, was also in action at this time, crushing a Turkish attempt to take El Kantara on the canal.

The Gurkhas are notable for their lively sense of humour and competition, as evidenced by this 'wrestling match' for men of the 1/1st King George's Own Gurkha Rifles on the battalion's pack mules. The match took place behind the lines in France during August 1915, shortly before the battalion was pulled out of the theatre.

The third battalion in the theatre was the 2/7th, which had seen no action since it was raised in 1908. However, the battalion was singled out for a novel task, namely an amphibious assault on Turkish-inspired Arab dissidents who were holding El Tur in the Gulf of Suez. Despite their lack of experience with amphibious operations, and the choppy state of the sea, the detachment of the 2/7th Gurkha Rifles was ferried in the protected cruiser HMS *Minerva* and put safely ashore on 11 February 1915. After a nine-mile approach march, the Gurkhas put in their attack on El Tur at dawn: by midday it was all over, and for the loss of one man the Gurkhas had killed 60 Arabs and captured another 100. The one Gurkha casualty was the first man of the 7th Gurkha Rifles ever to have been killed in action, and he was buried with extraordinary ceremony: a firing party of the Royal Marines and flags at half-mast on all Royal Navy warships in the area. As the regimental historian put it: 'It is improbable that any Gurkha Rifleman has even been, or will ever be again, attended to his grave with so much honour.'

Of the three battalions mentioned above, the 1/6th and 2/10th Gurkha Rifles were now destined for the dreadful Gallipoli campaign while the 2/7th Gurkha Rifles were earmarked for the Mesopotamia campaign. The story of the ill-fated Gallipoli venture has been adequately covered in a number of useful works, so it suffices here to say that the whole venture was schemed in its essential features by Winston Churchill, at the time the First Lord of the Admiralty, as a means of driving Turkey out of the war in one fell swoop. The basic plan was for an Allied naval squadron to crush any units of the small Turkish navy that might intervene and push through the Dardanelles, the Sea of Marmora and the Bosphorus to Istanbul, the arrival of the Allied squadron in the midst of the Turkish capital being expected to cause an immediate Turkish surrender and so open up a maritime route for the easy support of a struggling Russia. The plan was bold and far-sighted, but perhaps too bold and not far-sighted enough, for the presence of shore batteries and minefields meant that the initial naval effort to force the Dardanelles was a failure.

Undeterred, Churchill pushed through a scheme for a joint venture: British and French troops would land simultaneously on the north (Gallipoli) and south (Chanak) sides of the Dardanelles to suppress the shore batteries, allowing minesweepers to clear the Dardanelles for the capital ships, which would then press on to Istanbul. The plan was strategically sound but operationally and tactically unsound, not least because the Allies were woefully ill-prepared for such an operation, and led by army commanders of the utmost timidity against poorly equipped Turkish forces led by two exceptional commanders, Mustafa Kemal (later Kemal Ataturk, founder of modern Turkey) and the German Liman von Sanders. Given these factors, the whole Dardanelles operation could not have succeeded, and the pity of the whole affair is that its initial phase worked just sufficiently well to encourage the Allies to persevere when it would have been better to concede immediate defeat and so withdraw without the ensuing months of bitter trench fighting and horrendous casualties. At the unit level, the Dardanelles campaign was conditioned by the fact that the Allies were able to get troops ashore, but not to push inland to secure a useful beach-head for sustained operations. Thus the campaign turned into a succession of bitterly-fought battles as the British, in particular, sought to fight their way off the beaches and cliffs immediately behind them, ultimately without success despite a further landing closer towards the neck of the Gallipoli peninsula that should have cut off the Turkish forces opposing the initial beach-head areas.

Such then was the Gallipoli campaign, which lasted from the first landings of 25 April 1915 to the final evacuation of 9 January 1916. This latter was carried out with consummate skill (perhaps the greatest example ever of the British ability to do things right only after complete failure), but total Allied losses had been 252,000 dead. The entire campaign, from the point of view of the fighting man, was horrendous as a result of the tactical situation, extreme heat together with a lack of drinking water, disease and poor terrain for fighting or surviving. From the Gurkhas' point of view, however, the situation was eased, though only very slightly, by the terrain's similarity to that encountered on the North-West Frontier.

This factor was recognized by the man designated to command the expedition, General Sir Ian Hamilton, who in March 1915 wrote to Kitchener, the

Once they were deployed to the right theatre and under the right conditions, the Gurkhas became by any standards truly formidable infantrymen in World War I, proving particularly adept at skirmishing and patrolling for offensive purposes.

Secretary of State for War, that 'Each little Gurkha might be worth his weight in gold at Gallipoli.' Thus three Gurkha battalions were allocated for the initial assault: the 1/5th, 1/6th and 2/10th Gurkha Rifles. None of these was involved in the actual landings on 25 April, the 1/6th Gurkhas of the 29th Indian Brigade being the first to arrive on 1 May, by which time casualties amounted to 3000 dead and 6000 wounded, and by which time early hopes for rapid success had evaporated. The 29th Indian Brigade was the reserve for the whole British assault force, which had landed on six beaches, so the units of the brigade, the Gurkhas included, had a hectic time of it during the next fews days as the Turks rushed up reinforcements to try to drive the British back into the sea.

The 6th Gurkhas moved into the line on 9 May, and were immediately entrusted with a key task, the capture of a commanding bluff that had already defeated efforts by the Royal Marines and Royal Dublin Fusiliers. The Turks had turned the summit of the bluff into a nest of machine-gun posts, and these had decimated the two previous attacks. The Gurkhas opted for another approach for their attack of 12 May: instead of attacking from below, as had done the Royal Marines and Royal Dublin Fusiliers, they would attack laterally across a ravine to take the top of the bluff before Turkish reinforcements could arrive. The plan succeeded admirably, the Gurkhas'

hill warfare experience standing them in good stead as the attention of the defence was distracted by a diversionary attack and naval gunfire support. Thus the bluff was taken with what were for the Gallipoli campaign only moderate casualties, namely 18 dead and 42 wounded. In honour of the occasion, the British named the feature Gurkha Bluff. There followed two months without major demands on the Gurkhas. Nevertheless, additional losses were suffered during the incessant round of raid and counter-raid carried out by both sides. With summer approaching the heat became a considerable problem, as did the plague of flies and disease emanating from the unburied corpses rotting in no man's land. In these circumstances it was inevitable that louse infestation should crop up, and that dysentery should become a major source of losses.

On 3 June the 2/10th Gurkhas joined the 1/5th and 1/6th Gurkhas in the 29th Indian Brigade, and though plans had not called for the Gurkhas' use in the 3rd Battle of Krithia, the dire situation called for the 1/5th and 1/6th Gurkhas both to be deployed. The latter battalion was called upon to undertake a neat ruse: at the signal, the men were to man their fire positions and suggest to the Turks that an infantry assault was imminent, so that a crushing artillery bombardment could be brought down upon the Turks as soon as they had come out from cover. Unfortunately the wire was not cut by the artillery, and the Turks had for the most part managed to find cover as the barrage came down, so that the advancing Gurkhas were met by a withering fire from rifles and machine-guns. Despite this, the battalion's C Company managed to reach its objective, then finding itself surrounded on three sides as no other units of the 29th Indian Brigade had managed to achieve their targets; there was no alternative but to pull back, though effective naval gunfire support prevented the Turks from inflicting heavy casualties on the Gurkhas. The whole campaign was run, on the Allied side at least, with a total lack of imagination and flair, and the 1/5th Gurkhas were ordered to repeat the exercise on the following day; inevitably, the Turks were waiting and savaged the battalion. Thereafter a temporary lull settled over the area for the rest of June, the three battalions just suffering the constant drain of disease and raiding party casualties as each side built up its strength.

On 28 June the pace speeded up again, the 29th Indian Brigade being tasked with driving the Turks back some 1000 yards to the north-west of Gurkha Bluff. This was the start of the Gully Ravine battle, which got under way with useful British advances but then stalled as the Turks threw in counterattack after counterattack. The battle raged for eight days before the line was restabilized after an 800-yard British advance. The Turks had lost some 10,000 casualties, but the 29th Indian Brigade too had been yet again mauled. The 2/10th Gurkhas, for example, had suffered 70 per cent officer and 40 per cent other rank losses during its five weeks on Gallipoli, most of these during the Gully Ravine battle. The brigade was thus pulled out for a month of recuperation and reinforcement on the island of Imbros.

The brigade and its three Gurkha battalions was then slated for a major role during the second-phase landings on Gallipoli, scheduled for 6 August 1915: the British force had been reinforced with another three divisions, and new landings were to be made at Suvla Bay closer to the neck of the peninsula to take the Turkish positions in flank while a major breakout effort was launched from the initial landing lodgement. The object of this latter was to take the dominating Sari Bair Ridge, and the 29th Indian Brigade was allocated the central feature of this ridge, Hill Q, as its objective for 7 August. The terrain for the brigade's attack is forbidding in the extreme, comprising an apparently endless succession of steep ravines liberally coated with prickly bushes. The brigade was also beset by inaccurate maps and the need to approach at night, and though these difficulties could have been mitigated by the use of Gurkhas for covert reconnaissance, this was forbidden.

Nevertheless the approach succeeded tolerably well, junior officers and NCOs showing considerable skill and flair in the positioning of their units. But then, for a reason never adequately explained, the Gurkhas were halted just short of their objective shortly before dawn. Orders had expressly forbidden such a halt, presumably because it was believed that the assault forces would reach this position only shortly before the scheduled assault time. Tragically, the Gurkhas and other battalions were thus prevented from attacking an unwary opposition at its most vulnerable time, with the inevitable consequence that the 10.30 attack met a fully prepared and ideally sited enemy: the result was a foregone conclusion, and despite the availability of naval gunfire support, the multi-national British force was most severely handled. A telling commentary on the casualties suffered is provided by a statement in the official history, to the effect that 'Seven and a half hours after scheduled time, the main attack by the right assaulting column whose strength on the spot amounted to four and a half battalions, was opened with five companies.' No. 3 Double Company of the 2/10th Gurkhas was particularly hard hit, and on the following day could muster only about 12 men. The Gurkhas and companion New Zealanders fought with monumental tenacity to drive up to the Turkish positions, but could make no headway against the zones of interlocking machine-gun fire.

By now it should have been clear that success was impossible, especially as the Turks would naturally reinforce their positions at the crest of the ridge features. But the British command refused to accept the obvious, with the result that further attacks were launched on 8 and 9 August. The Gurkhas were heavily engaged in both of these attacks (in the latter because a British brigade coming to relieve them got lost in the ravine area), and again suffered heavy losses: the 10th Gurkhas were reduced to some 200 men. Perhaps the greatest and most ironic tragedy of the whole battle, which cost the Allies some 12,000 casualties, was that the Gurkhas did manage to reach and seize a strategic crest position: a relatively small party of the 6th Gurkhas stormed a Turkish position after it had been devastated by naval gunfire, and

The headquarters of the 1/1st Gurkhas in northern France during August 1915.

after a savage 10-minute close-quarter action with bayonets and kukris killed or drove off the remnants of the Turkish defence. The tragedy lay in the fact that naval gunfire was called down on the crest as it was assumed that the Turks were still in control, forcing the Gurkhas to pull back to their position some 200 ft from the crest. Thus a small party of Gurkhas were the only British troops to obtain the marvellous view from the top of Sari Bair Ridge during World War I, and the extreme exhaustion of the British forces then made inevitable a general withdrawal from the area. The 6th Gurkhas, it should be noted, had lost all their British officers, leaving Subadar Major Gambirsing Pun in command, though he had to communicate with command by means of the battalion's medical officer who had the necessary English and Gurkhali.

The landings at Suvla Bay had continued the British ineptitude in the theatre: initially un-opposed, the landings had at first gone smoothly, but then the local commander halted his troops well short of the dominating heights above Suvla Bay. The Turks rushed in two divisions to secure the heights, and then pushed the British back virtually to the beaches. A golden opportunity had again been lost, leaving the Brtish with yet another mere toehold on Gallipoli.

Hamilton realized, however, that the Suvla beach-head offered the greatest chance for a break-out, and so reinforced the divisions there with the highly experienced 29th Division from the Cape Helles beach-head. With this division went the much depleted 29th Indian Brigade, which was selected to spearhead the offensive scheduled for 21 August in an effort to relieve the Turks of the high ground at the western side of Suvla Bay. Well prepared, well dug-in and in full possession of the commanding ground, the Turks savaged the attack without mercy, and yet again a British offensive stalled on the slopes of the objective, producing yet another site for the development of trench warfare. Yet the campaign dragged on remorselessly, each day seeing a trickle of casualties from operational or disease reasons. Neither side could make progress, and then the winter arrived. All suffered horribly in the intense cold and wet, and the Gurkha battalions were reduced to about 100 men each. Hamilton had been relieved of his command in October, and the new commander swiftly realized that all that could be achieved was a careful evacuation. The 10th Gurkhas were pulled out before the end because of their losses: 240 men were buried on Gallipoli, and of the original battalion that had sailed from Alexandria only one officer and 79 Gurkhas returned.

The whole Dardanelles operation had been a fiasco, and was generally characterized by two features that frequently cropped up in World War I, namely the ineptitude of many senior commanders, and the courage and capability of the ordinary soldier. And amongst such ordinary soldiers on Gallipoli none did better than the Gurkhas.

While the Gallipoli affair was being fought out in the blood of ordinary soldiers, Gurkhas were also becoming embroiled in the other Middle Eastern campaigns, those for Palestine and Mesopotamia. Both were in grand strategic terms relative sideshows to the climactic campaigns waged in Europe, but nevertheless of great local significance: British success was essential for the safeguarding of oil supplies and the route to India and the Far East, while joint Turkish and German success could sway the Moslem world against the British. Mesopotamia was run operationally by the government of India, and in this fact lay the reason for the gradual expansion of the campaign's rationale from local protection for the southern Persian oilfields (and of the associated pipelines and ports) to a more ambitious scheme to extend British domination into Mesopotamia at least as far as Baghdad. It was felt that Turkish opposition would be slight, and that far-reaching political goals could be achieved with little expenditure of men and money. How wrong the Indian government was. Yet there was to be a campaign, and at various times substantial numbers of Gurkhas were involved, initially under the overall

command of General Sir John Nixon, who saw a golden opportunity stretching ahead of him after the simple capture of Basra in December 1914 at the start of the campaign.

The first Gurkha unit to arrive in Mesopotamia was the 2/7th Gurkha Rifles, which was shipped from Egypt soon after its successful foray at El Tur. In Mesopotamia it was allocated to the 9th Indian Division commanded by Major General Charles Townsend, who organized a portion of his division as the infantry component of the amphibious flotilla despatched up the River Tigris in pursuit of the Turks withdrawing after their loss of Shaiba towards Nasiriya. The 7th Gurkhas were amongst the units allocated to the flotilla, which had an extraordinarily difficult time of it: in parts the Tigris was nothing more than a vast swamp, and the boats had to be dragged through and over these conditions by main force; disease was also a major problem right from the start, and the Gurkhas were soon reduced from some 800 to 350 in strength, most of the losses being attributable to heat stroke and malaria. The Battle of Nasiriya was fought on 24 July 1915, and the 7th Gurkhas distinguished themselves in this, their first major action. Yet for a moment the outcome of the battle was in the balance until a Gurkha corporal charged a Turkish position with his kukri, followed by his section. The deaths of 13 Turks encouraged the remainder of the British force, and the Turks were swept from the battlefield. Unfortunately for the British campaign in Mesopotamia, this success also convinced Townsend that further advance was in order, certainly as far as Kut-al-Amara at the junction of the Rivers Tigris and Euphrates. Whitehall reluctantly permitted Delhi to authorize this advance, and so was set in motion the course of events that were to embroil British and Indian forces for the rest of World War I.

Townsend reached Kut with some 11,000 men, and on 28 September succeeded in capturing the town after a smart action characterized by neat tactical ploys but only limited use of Gurkhas. However, the Turks fell back towards Ctesiphon, where a major defensive position was being prepared by an increasingly determined Turkish command. But reinforced by the 3rd Lahore and 7th Meerut Divisions from France, Townsend was determined to press on and again secured the necessary authorization from Delhi and London. Underestimating the strength and determination of the Turks, Townsend pressed on to engage a powerful Ottoman force at Ctesiphon on 22 November 1915: the battle raged for four days before Townsend would admit that the injection of Turkish reserves made the British position untenable, and he then ordered a withdrawal to Kut. Townsend had overreached himself at Ctesiphon, for his tactical plan called for carefully co-ordinated attacks by four separate columns whose adequate strength could only be ensured by the foregoing of any central reserve. The Gurkhas formed part of the column under General Delamain, and had to cross some 5000 yards of open desert to storm its objective. The battalion ran into uncut wire, however, and suffered heavy casualties before it could press through to its objective.

Such had been the losses of the Gurkhas and accompanying Dorsets that a Turkish counterattack drove them out again, but it was on the next day that the 7th Gurkhas really excelled themselves, under extremes of heat and plagued by flies. Some 300 men of the battalion, with a party of the 21st Punjabis, were to defend a small mound close to the Arch of Ctesiphon, and this mound later became known as Gurkha Mound in honour of the defence of this feature against the Turkish 35th Division, which failed to dislodge the Gurkhas and Punjabis and suffered very heavy losses. As one of the Turkish officers later wrote, 'I must confess to a deep hidden feeling of appreciation for that brave and self-sacrificing enemy detachment which, though only 400 strong, for hours opposed the thousands of riflemen of the 35th Division.' The Battle of Ctesiphon cost the Gurkhas some 30 per cent of their strength, 62 dead and 200 wounded, yet these losses were relatively light in comparison with those of other units. The inevitable conclusions should have been that the Turks were neither as inept nor as demoralized as Townsend and his advisers had confidently claimed, and that if the British were to succeed in Mesopotamia far greater efforts would be needed.

Kut was soon besieged by the Turks, and as Townsend signalled that he would defend Kut as he had defended Chitral, Nixon organized a relief force under General Fenton Aylmer. In this latter was the 1/2nd Gurkha Rifles, newly arrived from India and wholly inexperienced in the type of warfare soon to be its lot. The battalion was blooded in the battle for the Dujailah Redoubt on 8 March 1916, right at the southern tip of the Turkish position encircling Kut. The Turkish forces included veterans of Gallipoli, and the 2nd Gurkhas were repulsed after losing 100 dead and 100 wounded. The reverse at the Jubailah Redoubt marked the end of the relief effort, and Kut thus fell to the Turks: the 2/7th Gurkhas received the honour of marching out under arms as the garrison surrendered its 8500 personnel. The disaster at Kut was compounded by a further 20,000 casualties amongst the relief force, and the repercussions of this defeat were to have strong effects on the Moslem world.

As the summer of 1916 advanced the British licked their wounds and built up reinforced strength for renewed action with 165,000 combat troops, two-thirds of them from the Indian establishment and including several Gurkha battalions. Command was now vested in General Sir Frederick Maude, and in September 1916 strategic responsibility for the Mesopotamian campaign was assumed by the War Office in London. The summer was not devoid of incident, however, for the Turks and local Arab leaders took the opportunity of British immobility for probing raids and the like, leading to a number of skirmishes and punitive raids by the British forces. In such operations the Gurkhas developed local skills and learned how best to live and survive in the exacting conditions of Mesopotamia. Additional casualties were incurred by the forces (including two Gurkha battalions, the 2/6th and 1/10th Gurkha Rifles) guarding the expeditionary force's relatively long and highly vulnerable lines of communication from Basra.

By December Maude judged that his one cavalry and five infantry divisions were ready for an offensive towards Baghdad: reorganization, reinforcement and resupply had combined with intensive training to improve the lot of the soldiers out of recognition, and also raised their morale by bringing them the realization that they were much improved in their basic military skills. The British forces moved off towards Kut once again on 13 December, the Gurkhas playing a key part in the reconnaissance and feint operations that convinced Maude that the Turks were dug in round Kut in determined mood.

It was clear that positional manoeuvring would not dislodge the enemy, and the British and Indian troops would have to undertake serious operations.

There followed a series of small-scale attacks, many involving the Gurkhas, as Maude probed the Turkish defences and prepared for the decisive encounter. Losses on both sides were heavy during this period, but several of the Turkish outposts were driven back, offering Maude the choice of several points for the assault crossing that would have to be made before Kut itself could be attacked. A major problem facing Maude was the fact that the Tigris was nearly double its normal width, at some 400 yards, because of recent rainstorms that had also increased the stream considerably.

The main battle was readied for 22 February 1917, and an important part was allocated to the 37th Brigade (including the 1/2nd and 2/9th Gurkha Rifles), which was tasked with crossing the Tigris some 6 miles upriver from Kut to close the Turks' escape route towards Baghdad. The scheme went awry at an early point, and the Gurkhas lost very heavily during their assault crossing. But the crossings were achieved, though these cost the 2nd Gurkhas 80 dead and 43 wounded, and the British forces then fought for the next two days to seize the bottleneck through which any Turkish escape would have to be made. Meanwhile the rest of Maude's force had launched the primary assault on Kut, the 2/7th Gurkhas raised to replace the battalion lost in the siege of Kut playing an important part. Bitter fighting raged for three days, but on 25 February the Turks decided to fall back while their escape route to Baghdad was still open. Though harried by the British cavalry, the Turks managed to get away in substantial numbers as the British and Indian infantry was too spent to pursue. The way was now open to Baghdad, which Maude's forces entered without opposition on 11 March after several days of severe fighting along the Diyala river. Both sides now paused, the desperate heat of the summer making sustained operations all but impossible.

Baghdad had been the primary target of the Delhi's government's ambitions in Mesopotamia, and with its capture the strategic objective of the campaign had been achieved. But the Turks still possessed substantial forces in the area, their main strength now being centred on Mosul. It was clear that sustained operations would be impossible during the intense heat of the summer months that were now upon the combatants, and the pace of operations was slowed as the British consolidated their current successes and planned for an advance on Mosul once cooler weather returned in the autumn. As well as the destruction of the last major Turkish forces in Mesopotamia, success in the Mosul area would bring under British control the area's rich oilfields.

But before standing down for the summer, the British sent out three columns to harass the retreating Turks, one each up the Tigris, Euphrates and Diyala rivers. On the Euphrates lies Ramadi, a major obstacle in any advance towards Mosul, and it was deemed advisable to take this position before the Turks could dig in during the summer. Entrusted with the task was the 7th Brigade, which included the 2/7th Gurkhas: the attack was a total failure because of climatic rather than military reasons. Short of water, and exhausted from several days of rapid advance, the units of the 7th Brigade were in no real state for an assault. Yet the units tried to attack, and the example of the 7th Gurkhas speaks volumes for the conditions, as by 14.30 no fewer than 250 Gurkhas had collapsed from the heat, being joined by some 60 battle casualties as the Turkish position was reached. The attack was called off, and the opposing forces settled down for a summer of heat.

With the advent of cooler weather in September, Maude was able to resume his offensive, and this time there was to be no failure at Ramadi, whose reduction was the responsibility of the 15th Indian Division, incorporating the 42nd Indian Brigade with the 1/5th, 2/5th and 2/6th Gurkha Rifles as well as the 1/4th Dorsets. These battalions moved up during the night of 25–6 September, and attacked at dawn against a clearly disheartened enemy. There were still some serious pockets of resistance, and indeed the 2/6th Gurkhas were completely pinned down on Ramadi Ridge after the Turkish flanks had been turned by other units, forcing the Turks to pull back. Early on the following morning the Turks surrendered, and the way was open to Mosul after further preparation. Fate intervened, however, as Maude died of cholera during November. His successor was General Sir William Marshall, but

Maude's offensive schemes were curtailed by altered strategic priorities and the need for further consolidation of the British lines of communication. Thus it was not until the closing stages of World War I that the Turkish forces in Mesopotamia were finally eliminated as part of the British scheme to crush the Ottoman empire with simultaneous blows in Palestine and Mesopotamia. The remnants of the Turkish Sixth Army were holding a main position at Sharquat on the route up the Euphrates to Mosul, and the task of ousting them was given to Indian I Corps commanded by Lieutenant General A.S. Cobbe. Cobbe planned carefully, and decided on simultaneous advances up both banks of the Euphrates to keep the Turkish commander unaware of the location of Indian I Corps' main strength. The 1/7th Gurkha Rifles were with the forces on the right bank of the river, while those on the left bank included the 1/10th Gurkhas. The Battle of Sharquat was the first time that the 1/7th Gurkhas had been under fire, and they performed admirably, showing extreme steadiness and being largely responsible for the Turkish withdrawal to their second line. With the Turks pinned by other units, the 1/7th Gurkhas and Guides Cavalry were despatched on an outflanking march of 36 miles (achieved in just 26 hours) to cut the Turks' line of retreat farther up the river. On the other bank of the Euphrates the 1/10th Gurkhas had no easier a time of it, for with other units the battalion was forced to fight through a succession of Turkish positions until the Turks fell back when their right flank broke. Thereafter a general battle followed as the Sixth Army strove to break out of the throng thrown round it by Marshall's forces. But there was to be no escape, and early on 29 October the Turkish commander surrendered his surviving forces.

The war in Mesopotamia was now all but over, and after a deal of squabbling the garrison of Mosul surrendered to Cobbe's cavalry on 14 November. But there remained one more task for the Gurkhas in this theatre, as there had existed in Persia for some time a considerable unrest heavily fanned by German agents. Among the British and Indian forces drafted into this country during 1917 and 1918 to quell any indications of active resistance to British efforts were the 1/2nd and 1/6th Gurkha Rifles, who had several brushes with the Jangali

guerrillas of Kuchik Khan: the first of these occurred in July 1918, and the Jangalis were soundly beaten by the Gurkhas, whose effective use of their kukris soon became something of a legend in the area. The Jangalis were not finally beaten until 1921, and the British forces finally left the country that January.

The other major theatre to witness the growing prowess of the Gurkhas was Palestine, scene of major operations by the 1st, 3rd, 7th and 8th Gurkha Rifles. After the repulse of the Turkish efforts in 1915 to sever Britain's shortest routes to India, the Far East and Australasia by capturing the Suez Canal, the British high command prudently decided that the best way in which to deny the Turks another opportunity to attack the canal was to take the campaign into the Sinai desert, where the establishment of a substantial British bridgehead would provide a buffer for the canal, and also a springboard for an offensive into Palestine and so up into southern Turkey.

Thus between January and July 1916 the British forces commanded by General Sir Archibald Murray drove deep into the Sinai against limited resistance, and established the network of water pipelines, supply dumps, communication networks and other paraphernalia for a sustained drive into Palestine. British preparations were little hampered when a Turkish force with German machine-gun support attacked the railhead at Rumani in August 1916, and by the end of the year the British had moved as far forward as El Arish.

Thereafter Turkish resistance strengthened considerably, and the British were sharply reversed in the first two battles of Gaza in March and April 1916. The local commander, General Sir Charles Dobell, was relieved by Murray, who was in turn replaced at the insistence of the War Office by General Sir Edmund Allenby, who was instructed to take Jerusalem before Christmas 1917. Allenby's new broom in Palestine was similar to that of Maude in Mesopotamia: commanders moved up to the front, organization and administration were streamlined, combat strength was built up (in this instance to seven infantry divisions and the Desert Mounted Corps) and a rigorous programme of tactical training was instituted.

That Allenby had struck the right note was clearly evidenced in the 3rd Battle of Gaza on 31 October

1917: while three divisions pinned down the Turks in Gaza itself, the Desert Mounted Corps swung into the Turks' rear at Beersheba to capture the all-important water supply. With their lines of communication all but severed, the Turkish armies pulled rapidly back towards the north, the Seventh Army falling back on Jerusalem and the Eighth Army retreating up the coast. The gap that thus opened between the two Turkish armies was swiftly exploited by Allenby, who sent the Desert Mounted Corps through the gap for the Battle of Junction Station on 13 November 1917. British success hastened the further retreat of the Eighth Army.

Allenby was now free to turn his attention to the Seventh Army and Jerusalem, which had been reinforced by the Turkish Yilderim Force (diverted from Mesopotamia) and now under the command of General Erich von Falkenhayn. There was much bitter fighting in the Judaean hills before Allenby's forces could close in on Jerusalem, which finally fell to the British on 9 December 1917. This triumphant success was followed by a stagnant pause of some nine months as Allenby's forces were drained to provide reinforcements for the climactic battles taking place on the Western Front, and by the need to divert small but nonetheless useful elements to support the Arab insurrection against the Turks in the Hejaz. By the summer, however, Allenby's forces were once again on the increase, while the rapid decline of the Central Powers made imperative an early offensive to extend Britain's sphere of influence as far into the erstwhile Ottoman empire as possible. By this time the Turks had deployed the Fourth, Seventh and Eighth armies in a well-sited and well-fortified line across Palestine from a point on the Mediterranean coast just north of Jaffa to the valley of the River Jordan; able command was provided by General Liman von Sanders. But Allenby had spent the summer in careful preparation for what was clearly to be a decisive blow during September.

This blow, which fell on the Turks on 19 September 1918, was the Battle of Megiddo: Allenby fielded 57,000 infantry, 12,000 cavalry and 540 guns against the Turks' 36,000 men and 360 guns. However, the main weight of the British forces was disposed with XXI Corps on the British left flank on the Plain of Sharon, where 35,000 infantry

(including four battalions of Gurkhas) and 400 guns were faced by only 8000 Turks and 130 guns. Allenby's plan, a masterpiece (in terms of planning and of execution) of fire and movement, was to punch through the Turkish right wing after a short but savage artillery bombardment to provide the Desert Mounted Corps with a gap through which it could stream into the Turkish rear areas, which were to be paralysed by the bombing of headquarters, dumps and railway junctions by aircraft of the Royal Air Force.

Typical of the efforts of the Gurkhas in this great battle was that of the 2/7th Gurkha Rifles, part of the 3rd Division. The battalion had arrived in Palestine during May 1918, and become acclimatized during a period of garrison and patrol duty in the Auja river area, where some 400 men were afflicted by a particularly virulent form of malaria; some 40 of the victims died. By September it was back to a good strength, and fully prepared for the offensive which started at 04.30 on 19 September. The battalion moved off with its companion units of the 3rd Division, and soon lost touch in the darkness while starting the wheeling movement that was to take the five divisions through the Turkish line. Yet the battalion pressed on regardless, commanders being fully confident of their map reading, and pushed through the Turkish front-line defences as ordered. The degree of confusion is evident from the fact that while the battalion was short of a few of its component units, it had gained platoons from other battalions which had become disorientated in the dark.

The 2/7th Gurkhas pressed on again deeper into the Turkish rear, and the success of this and other battalions paved the way for the three cavalry divisions of General Chetwode's Desert Mounted Corps to pass through. The Turkish Eighth Army disintegrated, the Seventh pulled back in disarray towards the Jordan, and the British swept on into Syria and forward towards Turkey proper. By the time that Turkey capitulated on 30 October 1918, the British forces had pushed through as far as Beirut, Damascus, Homs and Aleppo. As its part in this rout, the 2/7th Gurkha Rifles advanced past Jezreel and Nazareth to the Sea of Galilee, the entire campaign having cost the battalion some 100 men.

It is also interesting to note that as Chetwode's

cavalry poured north towards Aleppo, it encountered a party of escaped prisoners-of-war, amongst them a group of the 2/7th Gurkhas captured in the fall of Kut. It was only with the release of men such as these that the horrors of life in Turkish prisoner-of-war camps finally began to emerge. Though at the time there was great British anger at the way in which the Turks had 'mistreated' their prisoners-of-war, it soon became clear that no ill-will had been evident, but rather the totally indifferent state of Turkish administration and supply, which had allowed Turks as well as prisoners-of-war to languish in remote spots without food, clothing and other essentials.

And so ended World War I. The Gurkhas had played a vital part in the eventual British success. First they had helped to restore the Allies' fortunes in France after the dark days of August and September 1914, and then they had moved to warmer climes as part of the great British effort in the eastern Mediterranean and Mesopotamia: Gallipoli tested the Gurkhas to the extremes of courage, skill and physical endurance, and found them not wanting; Mesopotamia examined their endurance and resilience, and again found them not wanting; and Palestine sought their tactical skills and overall military virtues, and found them there in abundance. The cost had been high for Nepal's sons, but a yet firmer bond had been established between the British and the Gurkhas.

Jungle training before the Far East war broke out.

BETWEEN
THE WARS

Throughout the period between the world Wars, the Gurkhas were actively involved in India's defence problems, one of the major thorns being Waziristan, where this machine-gun post of the 1/3rd Gurkhas was hotly emplaced and embroiled during the late 1930s. The weapon is a Vickers water-cooled heavy machine-gun, used for long-range suppression with the aid of a rangefinder (under the elbow of the right-hand man).

Top left: Frontier operations were made all the more difficult as the opposition did not consist of a uniformed enemy, but a mass of tribesmen who, in adverse conditions, melted into the mass of innocent noncombatants. Here Gurkha riflemen guard a group of suspects for interrogation and possible release.

Left. The Gurkhas have consistently paid great attention to recruit training of all kinds, and here a party of recruits practises bridging techniques under the critical but encouraging eyes of NCOs of the 1st Battalion, 5th Gurkha Rifles.

Inevitably, the 'war to end all wars' could not and did not achieve any such thing, and though the Gurkha battalions slowly returned from Palestine and Mesopotamia (the last coming from Persia only in 1921) to India, there was little respite for them in a continent racked by a mass of internal and external problems. And with ineluctable certainty, the local area that caused the most trouble was the North-West Frontier with Afghanistan. Right through World War I the Afghan government had been placated by the payment of massive subsidies and checked by a relative indifference to the area on the part of Russia, but with the end of World War I the subsidies ceased and the new Soviet regime in Russia again stretched attention to the region. Thus the North-West Frontier required constant military attention, and in the years between the two world wars all 10 permanent Gurkha regiments saw service on this frontier, as did the three battalions of the 11th Gurkha Rifles, which had been raised for service in the Middle East during World War I.

Trouble with Afghanistan flared in 1919 after the assassination of the Amir Habibullah, who had maintained a strict neutrality throughout World War I for the subsidies given him by the British. Dissatisfied with this, and with the termination of the subsidies in 1919, a radical faction murdered the amir and put on the throne his third son Amanullah. Less than three months after his assumption of power, the Amir Amanullah proclaimed a *jehad* (holy war) against the British, whose administration in India was sorely beset by several internal problems as it sought to demobilize the 1,400,000 Indians who had volunteered for service with the British in World War I. Amanullah clearly expected to be able to raid with success against negligible opposition, and then to retire into Afghanistan without trouble. Thus no sooner had the *jehad* been declared than Afghan levies streamed across the border near Landi Khana to seize the town of Bagh on 3 May. But the British had no intention of letting the Afghans get away with so blatant a piece of opportunism, and so started the 3rd Afghan War. A punitive expedition was immediately organized, this comprising regular Indian army battalions including several of Gurkhas. The expedition's first take was the recapture of Bagh, on 3 May, followed by an advance to Landi Kotal in the Khyber Pass. There followed a push through the Khyber Pass towards Dakka, and aircraft of the Royal Air Force supplemented this effort by bombing Kabul and Jalalabad. Amanullah sued for peace on 31 May, fully realizing his initial error and the impossibility of stemming so determined a riposte by modern and combat-experienced troops. There was no general engage-

ment in the 3rd Afghan War, which was ended formally by the Treaty of Rawalpindi in August 1919, but rather a succession of forced marches (many by night) as the British sought to pin down and defeat small groups of Afghan forces.

The Treaty of Rawalpindi did not (and could not) treat the root causes of the 3rd Afghan War, and this was made abundantly clear by the continued raiding that characterized the 'peace' on the North-West Frontier for the next 20 years or so. Further evidence of the influence of the Afghans was felt in November 1919, when the Afghans expressed their annoyance with the end of the British subsidy by inciting a revolt in Waziristan. Here the Masudis were actively encouraged by the Afghans in a series of excesses that inevitably brought British retribution in the form of a punitive expedition of 30,000 men including Gurkha battalions and led by General

Looking extremely fit and highly capable (which he would most certainly have been after years of intermittent operations on the North-West Frontier), this machine-gunner of the 10th Gurkha Rifles provides an indication of the heavy machine-gun fire support that could be provided by a skilled man with a Vickers water-cooled gun.

The machine-gun section of a battalion of the 5th Royal Gurkha Rifles parades in service order together with its mules in about 1936. Constant operations and intensive training had by this time produced units at a peak of fitness and tactical capability, well able to develop into the formidable units they were called upon to become in World War II.

S.H. Climo. As this force was concentrating on the Tank Zam in mid-December 1919 it was attacked by the Masudis, who stook little chance against the disciplined firepower of the punitive expedition and were repulsed with heavy losses. This permitted Climo's force to move about Waziristan with little hindrance as it cleared up the surviving remnants of the revolt by February 1920. Yet again the Gurkha battalions were called upon to move swiftly over considerable distances in the normal routine of trying to pin down rebel bands before they could stash their weapons and fade into the background of regular tribal life. It was an extremely difficult undertaking with little chance of success, but kept the battalions on their toes in terms of fitness, ability to move rapidly and far, and basic tactical skills and weapon training.

Despite the continued occurrence of border disputes and internal rebellions, the rundown of the Indian army after World War I continued, and by 1921 all the Gurkha regiments were in India, the 11th Gurkha Rifles had been disbanded, and so too had the third battalions raised by all but the 4th and 10th Gurkha Rifles of the permanent establishment.

One of the many new techniques and devices with which the Gurkhas had to become accustomed during the period between the world wars was radio, and this set seems to have been an item of curiosity to men of the 1/3rd Gurkhas as late as 1936 in this illustration from operations in the Khaisdra valley on the North-West Frontier.

World War II saw an enormous increase in the number of Gurkhas serving in the Indian Army, and despite losses of more than 20,000 killed and wounded, there was never a shortage of recruits, such as these newcomers to the 4th Prince of Wales's Own Gurkha Rifles in 1940.

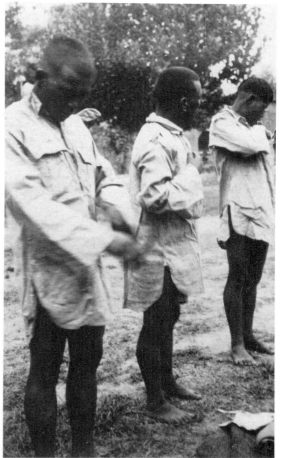

The time was now ripe for a thorough re-examination of the Indian army's tactical doctrines in the light of experience in World War I, and also the formal introduction of equipment and other items developed during the war. Thus the Gurkha regiments joined other units of the Indian army in exercises designed to promote practical co-operation with armoured vehicles and aircraft, while field exercises provided practical experience with 'new-fangled' equipment such as radio, motor transport and such weapons as mortars. The cycle to which the Gurkha regiments worked was a six-year one, with two years on the North-West Frontier followed by

four years in its cantonment area. However, the two-year period of active service on the frontier was often not followed by the four-year second-line period, for while the North-West Frontier remained the Indian government's primary military worry, there were large numbers of incidents that required military attention for their solution or, if possible, prevention. These thankless tasks fell to units not on active service, and included tours by various battalions of the Gurkha Brigade on the Malabar coast (1921–2), in the Moplah rebellion (1921), in Waziristan again (1925), in Burma (1930–2), and in the Bengal emergency (1932–4).

This was all grist to the Gurkha mill. For the Gurkha riflemen such diversions from the regular round of cantonment life were at times popular, especially as the average rifleman concerned himself little with the underlying reasons for any disturbance he was sent to quell: far more important to

Relatively light and delivering adequate quantities of high explosive over the short ranges possible in the jungle, mortars were ideally suited to the nature of the campaign in Burma. Here Gurkhas train with a 3-in mortar in the fraught but peaceful days of October 1941.

Gurkha training for jungle operations was undertaken in the period before World War II, but it had not been appreciated how swift and how quiet the men would have to be in order to defeat the Japanese.

such a man was the chance to put his skills to the test, to demonstrate his capabilities and, if the opportunity arose, to prove his courage under fire. This last was particularly important, for the ability to show off medals in his home village while on leave was important to the individual rifleman, and also a valuable aid to recruitment. Such activities were also vital in the life of the battalions, for it made it possible for subalterns who had joined their units in World War I to get to know their men under adverse conditions, developing a high degree of mutual trust and respect in the process, and to develop the skills of leadership over a period in which a substantial proportion rose to field rank and higher command. It cannot be denied that there were faults in the process, for India was a relative backwater where the development of tactics involving modern weapons was concerned, but what cannot be denied is that practical soldiering on the North-West Frontier and in civil disturbances made the Gurkha battalions magnificent units in terms of the type of warfare demanded of them.

Life was nevertheless good for the Gurkhas, for most of them were doing what they wanted in the way they liked it. There were inevitably grumbles: the pay for a rifleman had been increased from 11 to 16 rupees per month, but this was still a relatively small sum for a skilled fighting man who was in theory a mercenary and therefore needing to send money home; and there was some dissatisfaction that compared with the period before World War I regimental life had changed for the worse as a fair degree of everyday power was shifted from the battalion commander to Delhi. These were little things, however, compared with the earthquakes that devastated large portions of eastern Nepal in 1934 and the Quetta area of India in 1935. The former was construed locally as the gods' anger that British aircraft had flown over Mount Everest, and seriously affected the regions from which the 7th and 10th Gurkha Rifles were recruited; and the latter devastated the cantonments of the 7th Gurkha Rifles, who were fortunately absent at the time.

Also noticeable during the 1930s was an increasing concentration on the new type of warfare: though relatively remote from western Europe and Japan, India and her soldiers could not but realize the way that the world was moving as it rearmed with masses

of modern weaponry, and the 1930s were thus marked by a series of large-scale manoeuvres and exercises, frequently as all-arms operations in preparation for another global conflict. What was needed now was a considerable expansion of the Gurkha forces, the provision of new equipment suitable for the modern battlefield, and a specific role. To these the Gurkhas could bring superb discipline and the confidence of soldiers who were well used to being under fire, and specific skills such as close-quarter ambush work and night patrolling.

In the event the Gurkhas proved that little was beyond them in the military field, and expansion certainly proved no problem: all 10 regiments doubled their strengths by raising third and fourth battalions, and when the 1st, 2nd and 9th Gurkhas each lost an entire battalion in the fall of Singapore, each raised a fifth battalion. This brought Gurkha strength in World War II to an exceptional 43 battalions. Further unit strength was added by two Gurkha garrison units comprising reservists and wounded, and by five special Gurkha training units formed to give recruits realistic experience of combat. And it must be added that yet again Nepal threw its weight behind Britain, providing eight battalions for service initially in India on internal security duties (so freeing Gurkha regiments for overseas deployment) and later in the Burma campaign. It has been estimated that by the end of World War II the equivalent of some 55 battalions were serving with the Indian army, this entirely volunteer strength coming from a country with a population of a mere eight million.

And so the Gurkha Brigade went to war, though it is worth noting that by 1939 some regiments had changed their names yet again: in numerical order the regiments were now the 1st King George V's Own Gurkha Rifles (The Malaun Regiment), the 2nd King Edward VII's Own Goorkhas (The Sirmoor Rifles), the 3rd Queen Alexandra's Own Gurkha Rifles, the 4th Prince of Wales's Own Gurkha Rifles, the 5th Royal Gurkha Rifles (Frontier Force), the 6th Gurkha Rifles, the 7th Gurkha Rifles, the 8th Gurkha Rifles, the 9th Gurkha Rifles, and the 10th Gurkha Rifles.

A Gurkha patrol advances along a stream during jungle training in October 1941.

Gurkhas poised for action in Burma.

WORLD
WAR II

As had happened in World War I, the Gurkha regiments of the Indian army soon found themselves deeply involved in the crisis of British arms in World War II. But whereas World War I had found the Gurkha regiments, in common with other units of the Indian army (and indeed with the armies of many 'more advanced' nations), little prepared for the scale and the very nature of the conflict, World War II found the Gurkhas at a peak of preparedness and capability: there were inevitably deficiencies in training and, especially, in equipment as a result of the Indian army's low standing in the British order of priorities, but the Gurkhas were in general combat-experienced, fit and highly motivated, and were in World War II used more for the role which suited their talents. Thus the Gurkhas were deployed to North Africa, the Middle East, Italy and the dreadful campaigns in Malaya and Burma. Overall casualties were comparable with those in World War I, totalling some 20,000 dead and wounded.

The deployment picture well illustrates the extent of the Gurkhas' overseas commitments, with the 1st Gurkhas operational in Burma; the 2nd Gurkhas widely used in Burma, Persia, the Western Desert, Italy, Greece and Malaya; the 3rd, 4th and 5th Gurkhas were divided in their attentions with battalions each in Italy and Burma; the 6th Gurkhas fielded four operational battalions, of which three served in Burma and the fourth in Persia, Iraq, Palestine and Italy; the 7th Gurkhas had the ill fortune to suffer a repeat of earlier history, for its 2nd battalion was captured in Tobruk (being replaced by a new battalion which served in Syria, Palestine and Italy before moving to Greece at the end of the war) while its 1st Battalion was deployed to Burma; the 8th and 9th Gurkhas each had battalions in Italy and Burma; and the 10th Gurkhas had battalions in Burma, as well as other components in Syria, Iraq, Palestine and Italy. Two additional units, the 25th and 26th Gurkha Rifles, were raised for wartime service, but these were disbanded almost immediately after the end of hostilities. And a de-

Gurkhas in their element, as men of the 8th Army move forward with rifle and kukri towards the 'African Maginot Line' defences of the Mareth Line on the borders of Libya and Tunisia during March 1943.

parture for the Gurkhas during the course of World War II was the allocation of the 3/7th Gurkha Rifles as the Gurkha component of the Indian Parachute Regiment.

Again there is little space in this relatively short volume for any detailed assessment of the Gurkhas' history in World War II, so it must be sufficient to pencil in some of the battalions' stories as an indication of the strenuous war fought by these capable hillmen, whose reputation increased steadily on both sides of the front lines as the war progressed.

As noted above, the Gurkhas served on two main stages of World War II: the Middle East and North Africa, culminating in the invasion of Italy and the climactic battles as the Allies slowly drove the Germans north through the country, and Burma where the British fought a magnificent campaign first to halt the offensive of the Japanese as they swept towards India after their triumph in Malaya, and then to drive the Japanese back out of Burma as a preparatory move before the re-invasion of Malaya. In both these contrasting theatres the Gurkhas proved themselves superb infantrymen, and though Field Marshal Slim's comment that 'The Almighty created in the Gurkha an ideal infantryman ... brave, tough, patient, adaptable, skilled in fieldcraft' was directed towards the Gurkha in Burma, it is equally valid for the Gurkha in North Africa and Italy. In both theatres the Gurkhas faced adversaries of great skill and considerable experience, and had also to contend with extremes of terrain and climate. The Middle East and North Africa were in a way comparable with the terrain of the North-West Frontier in their dry climates marked by extreme heat by day and considerable cold by night, while Italy offered similar conditions often transformed into freezing, miserable sloughs of mud during the winter months, especially in the mountains. Burma, on the other hand, offered extremes of heat and humidity in a terrain characterized by alternating bands of jungle-covered mountain and savannah-like river plains as the British Fourteenth Army fought its way back to

With the poised confidence of the victors, a patrol of Gurkhas moves into Rangoon during May 1945. Among the weapons are two rifles, two Sten guns and one Bren gun, offering the patrol a potent and versatile firepower for a diversity of threats.

This artist's impression conveys the violence and speed of the 2/4th Gurkhas' capture of Point 132 above the Senio river in Italy during 1944, the kukri being used to good effect once the Gurkhas had closed with the Germans and their comparatively clumsy bayonetted rifles.

the Irrawaddy and then south towards Rangoon. Burma was also notable for the prevalence of endemic diseases such as malaria to compound the health problems of soldiers fighting in an area of extreme humidity and heat and little supported by the paraphernalia of modern medicine. Yet throughout these campaigns the Gurkhas coped with heat and cold, torrential rain and total aridity, and the rigours of nature and implacable human foes, displaying great fortitude and indeed cheerfulness, and throughout remaining effective combat infantrymen.

The 2/7th Gurkhas went to war in the first months of 1941, being warned for service in Persia and Iraq, which were both vital to the continued supply of oil to Britain as in World War I. The importance of these countries was also compounded by the fact that they formed essential links in British communications with the Far East and Australasia, and also in the overland communications with the southern USSR. This latter was to become increasingly important in the middle of 1941 when Germany invaded the USSR, which soon asked for and received substantial quantities of military aid and equipment from Britain and, increasingly, the USA. It was little surprising, therefore, that the Germans actively fomented trouble in the area: in May 1941 the Iraqi regime of Rashid Ali rebelled against the British administration with German support, and soon after this increasingly pro-German stances were taken by the Persian government. Thus when the 2/7th Gurkhas arrived at Basra in May 1941 they found themselves in the opening moves of a small but nonetheless lethal shooting war. Basra and the area upriver of this vital port were soon secured by the units of the Indian army in the region, leaving the major task of relieving Habbaniya, the British administrative and military headquarters in Iraq, which lies close to Baghdad and had been invested by the Iraqis.

The Gurkhas were allocated to the 10th Indian Division commanded by Major General William

Slim, and this force moved rapidly north to relieve
the Habbaniya garrison and crush the Iraqi revolt.
There remained the problem of Persia, which was
technically a neutral but was of far too great a
strategic importance to be ignored by the Allies, the
British moving in from the south and west and the
Soviets from the north to secure the overland route
to the USSR from the Persian Gulf. By this time the
2/7th Gurkhas had been joined in the theatre by the
1/2nd Gurkhas and the 2/10th Gurkhas. Little
resistance was encountered by the Indian and
Gurkha battalions in the area, and the campaign was
ended with little bloodshed. In strategic terms the
area had been secured for the Allied cause, however,
and in tactical terms the Iraqi and Persian operations
served as a useful introduction to the warfare of
considerable movement that would characterize
operations in the remaining Middle Eastern and
North African campaigns in which the Indian
army's forces were soon to be embroiled.

The 1/2nd Gurkhas and 2/7th Gurkhas were soon
after the end of the Persian campaign drafted to the
4th Indian Division commanded by Major General
Tuker. The 1/2nd Gurkhas were at first sent into
Cyprus, an island with few defences and which could
well have been the target for a German airborne
landing in succession to that on Crete as a further
step in Germany's move towards the Middle East
and southern USSR. Here the battalion was soon
engaged in strengthening the fixed and mobile
defences, while the 2/7th Gurkhas were moved into
North Africa as part of the 11th Indian Brigade.

In this theatre the see-saw campaign of Axis then
Allied predominance was once again witnessing a
period of German ascendency as the Eighth Army
was driven back towards the border of Egypt. Local
commanders had no intention of holding Tobruk as
they had done so magnificently in 1940 and 1941,
especially as in 1942 the Royal Navy felt that it could
not offer the same measure of support, but then

*During World War II, the Gurkhas proved themselves
most capable of adaptation into modern infantrymen for the
mechanized battlefield, and this capacity is exemplified in
this illustration of men of the 1/6th Gurkhas moving into
action against the Japanese near Singu on the Burma front
during February 1945 together with an M5 Stuart light
tank.*

Winston Churchill intervened to demand the retention of Tobruk, which had become a household term in Britain after its previous retention. But this time there was little chance to stockpile weapons, ammunition, food and the other requirements of war, and the garrison was restricted to the 2nd South African Division and the 11th Indian Brigade, the latter including the 2/7th Gurkhas.

The position was thus impossible when the siege started in June 1942: the South Africans were inexperienced, the fixed defences of the previous siege had been largely dismantled for use elsewhere,

November 1944, and a column of men from the 2/6th Gurkhas advances past a column of halted Bren Gun Carriers north of Tassello on the Italian front. The Gurkhas were well able to deal with the precipitous terrain and frequent cold of the Italian theatre, and were highly respected by the Germans for their tactical capabilities.

and the artillery and armour allocated to the garrison commander were woefully inadequate. The German blow fell on the 11th Indian Brigade, whose 2/5th Mahrattas were virtually destroyed as the German armour and infantry punched through the break opened by artillery and Stuka dive-bombers. The Germans and Italians then pushed on towards the port of Tobruk behind the overlarge defensive perimeter, this onslaught being hotly contested by the 11th Indian Brigades two flank battalions, the 2nd Cameron Highlanders and the 2/7th Gurkhas. Both battalions fought with considerable courage and skill, but they lacked the heavy weapons to inflict decisive damage on the Axis advance, and were soon reduced to the bayonet and kukri as small arms ammunition was exhausted. Company after Gurkha company was forced to concede defeat, and for the second time in little more than one-quarter of a

century the 2/7th Gurkhas were captured as a unit. A few men managed to evade the Axis net and regain the British lines, and quite remarkably it was again decided to permit the re-formation of the battalion from these survivors and fresh drafts from India, still within the 4th Indian Brigade.

The fall of Tobruk and the Axis forces' final push to the Egyptian frontier marked the high point of German fortunes in North Africa, though this was little appreciated at the time. Yet a new brush had arrived in the form of General Bernard Montgomery to head the Eighth Army, and while the British awaited Rommel's next offensive with trepidation, Montgomery set about restoring the morale and

A warmly kitted Gurkha pins down a German position with fire from his Thompson sub-machine gun somewhere on the Italian front during the closing stages of World War II.

matériel of the Eighth Army. In August the 7th Indian Brigade, including the 1/2nd Gurkhas, arrived in Egypt as part of the 4th Indian Division. Yet even before the battalion had moved into the line it suffered the regiment's worst ever single-day casualties when on 28 August, 68 men of the headquarters company were killed as an instructor inadvertently detonated a mine in their midst during a demonstration. Fortunately the battalion had one month in which to recover and produce a tithe of new headquarters specialists before the opening of the climactic Battle of El Alamein; other Gurkha battalions were generous in their offers of help, and new personnel arrived from India.

Montgomery's plan for El Alamein hinged on the infantry and armour of XXX Corps at the northern end of the Allied line, so the Gurkhas of XIII Corps played only a subsidiary role in this decisive battle.

Though subsidiary, this role was nonetheless important, for the infantry units of XIII Corps were tasked with pinning down and unhinging the German and Italian units to the south of the decisive coastal area to prevent Rommel receiving reinforcements once the decisive point had been reached. The Gurkhas played their part to perfection, and the Italians of the 'Brescia' and 'Folgore' Divisions were effectively held. As the Axis position began to disintegrate, the 4th Indian Division took a substantial number of prisoners: the 1/2nd Gurkhas, for example, took some 2000 Italians including two generals. The Eighth Army now launched a rapid pursuit of the retreating Axis forces, and much to the chagrin of the Gurkhas the 4th Indian Division was one of those left temporarily behind for lack of adequate motor transport.

Thus it was not until early 1943 that the division rejoined its front-line companions. The division arrived just in time for the Battle of the Mareth Line in March 1943, but was again allocated a secondary task, that of moving through the Matmata Moun-

Gurkhas launch a kukri charge, much feared by any opposition with whom the Gurkhas could close, for in hand-to-hand combat the kukri is a truly formidable personal weapon.

Another facet of modern warfare relatively novel to the Gurkhas was urban fighting and the ghastly business of house-clearing, yet these two Gurkha riflemen seem full of competence on the Italian front in January 1944.

tains on which the south-western end of the Axis line was hinged to outflank the Axis position and so trap the German and Italian divisions once the main breakthrough had been achieved on the coastal strip. Things did not work out as anticipated, for the breakthrough of the 50th Division on the coast was held by the Germans, this persuading Montgomery into a change of plan whereby the New Zealand Corps and 1st Armoured Division were sent on an extremely wide outflanking march to the south to cross the Matmata Mountains and then debouch through the Tebaga Gap in the Axis forces' rear. This diversion found the 4th Indian Division already deep in the highest part of the Matmata Mountains, the Gurkhas proving themselves highly adept at mountain warfare despite the German use of minefields. Nevertheless the 4th Indian Division took its two allocated passes over the Matmata Mountains, and their commander assured his men that such experience would undoubtedly prove useful in the future. Tuker can have had little realization how prophetic were his words.

The first indication of this came only a fortnight later, in the Battle of Wadi Akarit, fought by the energetic Rommel on a good choice of ground where the defence could be weighted on the coastal plain with its south-western extremity anchored on the Djebel Fatnassa massif. Montgomery again planned a decisive breakthrough on the coastal strip with British infantry backed by artillery, but Tuker persuaded Montgomery that Rommel must by now

be expecting such a tactic and that it would therefore be better to switch the centre of the assault to the south-west, where the 4th Indian Division would take the Fatnassa heights in a night assault to permit the Eighth Army to punch through in a wheeling movement behind Rommel's rear. Tuker then allocated the primary role in his attack to the 1/2nd Gurkhas and the 1/9th Gurkhas, who were to take the very pinnacle of the Fatnassa location in a silent night attack so that the 7th and 5th Indian Divisions could move through the passes below to start the wheeling movement. The whole assault was performed with beautiful precision as the two Gurkha battalions moved up into the hills without detection and closed in on their objectives. When the approach of the Gurkhas was finally detected, the Nepalese hillmen moved with astounding speed to assault and overrun their objectives, completely unsettling the

Axis defence as the two Italian divisions in the sector were penetrated.

Undoubtedly the highlight of the assault was the performance of Subedar Lalbahadur Thapa, second in command of D Company, 1/2nd Gurkhas. The company had been tasked with the capture of the highest point in the battalion's area, and this could be approached only up a steep path defended by several Italian picket positions. Lalbahadur and his men rushed through several of these pickets, killing the defenders as they went, until at the last picket before the summit the party was reduced to Lalbahadur and a mere two riflemen; little deterred, these three men charged the last position, killed several of the defenders and drove off the survivors before seizing the crest. Lalbahadur was immediately awarded the Victoria Cross for outstanding courage and exemplary leadership. Rommel swiftly appreciated the danger to his entire defensive line represented by this Gurkha success, and threw in a powerful counterattack during the next day, ably supported by German artillery firing over open sights. But the Gurkhas were in their element in such circumstances, managed to keep in touch with each other and with the divisional artillery, and so repulsed this despairing effort by the Germans, for whom total defeat in North Africa was now only a question of weeks.

As the Allies moved steadily forward towards Tunis against German resistance that may have weakened but never faltered, the 4th Indian Division was switched from the Eighth to the First Army in the centre of the Allied line. The division moved over 200 miles with other formations of the Eighth Army and went straight into action on arrival on 5 May 1943 as part of V Corps: the corps broke through straight towards Massicault and Tunis, and the war in North Africa was soon over. The Wadi Akarit battle had brought to the Gurkhas a considerable public prominence, but while the bulk of the British and American forces triumphant in North

Gurkhas dig themselves in on a patch of burned-out forest on the Burma front, the kukri being put to good use by the man sharpening stakes for the revetment. The date is 1944, when the Gurkhas had secured for themselves a clear position as some of the most capable and courageous infantry available to the Fourteenth Army.

With a grenade more than ready to hand, a Gurkha leads his companions up a jungle path in Burma during 1943. With swift ruthlessness, the Gurkhas had quickly appreciated the superiority of Japanese tactics in the jungle, and then adopted and adapted them into classic movement and ambush tactics.

Lance-Naik Dumbar Bahadur Sunwar inspects the remnants of a Japanese defensive bunker taken by men of the 3/10th Gurkhas during the bitter fighting for Scraggy Hill in the south-east corner of the Fourteenth Army's defensive perimeter round Imphal during 1944.

alterations to plan as a result. But by December 1943 the Allies were firmly held in front of the immensely strong Gustav Line along the line of the Garigliano and Sangro rivers. The natural strength of this line across Italy had been reinforced by German defensive works, and a bitter Italian winter was also playing its part in halting the Allies. And at the centre of this massive line was Monte Cassino, a precipitous height dominating the main west coast road to Rome and surmounted by the beautiful and ancient monastery of Monte Cassino. Here the XIV Panzer Corps of the German Tenth Army had halted the Allies in their tracks, an ominous portent for the future of the Italian campaign, which had been schemed by the Allies as a means of sucking in substantial numbers of German divisions as the Allies swept north. Instead it was becoming clear that in Italy the Germans, despite the defection of their Italian allies in September 1943, would be able to pin down many Allied divisions with a relatively few of their own, and with little draw on the decisive Eastern and imminent North-West Fronts.

Into this mess arrived the first Gurkhas in December 1943 as part of the 4th Indian Division. Conditions on the ground were appalling, and the very narrowness of the front meant that neither side could indulge in manoeuvre warfare, resulting in the type of attrition warfare so dreadfully reminiscent of World War I. The 4th Indian Division was initially allocated to Montgomery's Eighth Army on the eastern side of the Appennine Mountains, but the deteriorating position of the US Fifth Army before Monte Cassino meant that the 4th Indian and 2nd New Zealand Divisions were soon switched to the US Fifth Army as the New Zealand Corps commanded by Lieutenant General Sir Bernard Freyberg.

Confident that air superiority provided them with a decisive edge, and despite the bloody repulse of several previous assaults, the New Zealand Corps was committed to battle in early February 1944 after a foothold had been gained on the lower slopes of the mountain by the US 34th Division. Tuker was unfortunately stricken down by disease at this time, but he had in mind a surprise outflanking movement rather than the artillery-supported frontal assault adopted by Freyberg in the absence of dissent. A key role was entrusted to the 1/2nd Gurkhas, who were to attack the German positions below the monastery

Africa immediately buckled down to preparations for the invasion of Sicily, the 4th Indian Division was pulled back to Egypt, and then to Palestine, Syria and Lebanon for intensive retraining as a light division specializing in mountain warfare. It was clear to all that the campaign in Italy would be prolonged, and that there would be much demand for mountain warfare troops. Tuker was determined that his division would be supreme in this task.

At first the Allied advance through Sicily and southern Italy had progressed relatively smoothly, albeit with some worries about the increase in German defensive capability and a number of

with the support of the 2/7th Gurkhas who were to
act as porters to ferry up ammunition and other
essential supplies for the 1/2nd Gurkhas, whose final
objective was the monastery itself. Allied intelligence remained convinced that the Germans were
using the monastery as an observation post and fire-
support base, and that great benefit would accrue
from the destruction of the monastery by Allied
bombers.

This attack duly started on 15 February, and the
monastery was soon knocked to pieces by the bombs.
But the Germans had not hitherto used the building,

though now they were able to move swiftly into an
ideal defensive position amongst the rubble.
Moreover, no surface attack had been co-ordinated
with the air attack, so that the Germans were not
only provided with additional defence but also
forewarned that an attack up the mountain would be
forthcoming. The result was an inevitable disaster
when the 1/2nd Gurkhas attacked on 18 February:
the leading waves were cut down by machine-gun
and small arms fire, and when the survivors attempted to find cover in the scrub under the walls
of the devastated monastery they found to their con-

No sooner had hostilities against Japan ceased than the Gurkhas found themselves with other men of the Fourteenth Army posted to regions hitherto occupied by the Japanese. Here a Gurkha rifleman ensures an orderly egress of surrendered Japanese troops from Bangkok in Siam, first to prisoner-of-war camps and then to repatriation.

Experienced, confident and fit, and now moderately well supplied and furnished with excellent air support, Gurkhas move forward in the Monywa area of Burma during 1945. Note the grenade-launcher over the muzzle of the rifle of the man one from the back.

tinued cost that this had been liberally dosed with booby traps and mines. The battalion was completely pinned down, and some 150 dead, missing and seriously wounded had been suffered. Further casualties had been suffered in considerable numbers by the 2/7th Gurkhas as its men sought with great courage and determination to keep their compatriots supplied with ammunition, food, water and medical requirements. Inextricably locked in the ruins of the monastery and its environs at the top of the mountain, neither side could call in any type of fire support, and the battle was fought in grisly

hand-to-hand fashion reminiscent of Gallipoli during World War I.

This abortive effort was called off, though the Gurkhas were retained for a second attack, planned for 24 February. The men of the New Zealand Corps were ready on the appointed date, but the weather was not, and for the next three weeks the Indians, Gurkhas, British and New Zealanders huddled in their jump-off positions in conditions of extreme cold, heavy winds, snow and rain. As if this were not enough, the Allies were also involved in the day-to-day (or rather night-to-night) round of patrols and artillery bombardments as the German defence sought to disrupt the Allies' plans.

The weather cleared sufficiently on 15 March for the Allied bombers again to paste the monastery before the 2nd New Zealand Division and 5th Indian Brigade launched the major assault; the 7th Indian Brigade with its Gurkhas was tasked with a holding role and the assault forces moved through the town and up the slopes of the mountain towards the monastery. Yet again the main attack was a total disaster, largely because of the bómbing of Cassino town, which again provided the German defence with ideal defensive positions through which it was impossible for armour to move and suicidal for infantry to progress without such support. Nevertheless some progress was made, and two Gurkha battalions, the 1/9th Gurkhas and the 2/7th Gurkhas, performed miracles of endurance and infantry skill in holding Hangman's Hill right under the monastery and in supporting the 1/4th Essex in its holding of Castle Hill. These two features were essential to any further Allied progress, and the Germans launched a series of most determined counterattacks in an effort to dislodge the British and Gurkhas.

But soon it became clear that no real progress could be made, and the 1/9th Gurkhas at the apex of the Allied advance were ordered to slip back into the main Allied lines as the attack was called off. The Gurkhas had been in action for nearly six weeks, together with their decimated companions of the New Zealand Corps. The natural resilience of the Gurkhas was not to be denied, however, and within a few days the 4th Indian Division was judged combat-fit once again. It was posted to the Adriatic sector of the Eighth Army's front, in the region of Orsogna as part of the British V Corps. Here the pace of operations could not compare with the adversities of the Cassino sector, but the strength and determination of the German resistance meant that a steady stream of casualties were suffered as the Allies pressed slowly forward through the Gustav, Führer-Senger and Caesar Lines. The German hold on southern and central Italy was finally prised open on 11 May 1944 when the Polish II Corps of the Eighth Army launched the decisive battle for Monte Cassino, finally driving through this decisive check-point by dint of overwhelming numbers and extreme fortitude. By 4 June 1944 the Allies had taken Rome, and the way to northern Italy seemed open.

But this was not the way in which Field Marshal Kesselring saw matters. His engineers were prepar-

Gurkhas board a Douglas Dakota before the start of the 2nd Chindit operation in 1944. Though much was expected of the Gurkhas, they did not in the event perform well in the 1st expedition during 1943 as they were split up into small parties and commanded by officers unaccustomed to Gurkha ways. Matters were better organized in the 2nd expedition.

ing massive fixed defences in the north as the Gothic Line, and he intended to fight skilful holding actions to buy time for these defences to be completed. Thus the Allied push to the north was seriously delayed, and suffered heavy losses, as the Germans made excellent use of the hills and forests of the region to lay ambushes and small tactical minefields where the Allies could be halted and then disrupted by mortar and artillery fire. The Germans were thus able to slip away to their next position northwards as the Allies disentangled themselves and after a cautious delay moved on once again. Throughout July and August 1944, therefore, the Gurkhas of the 4th Indian Division fought their way north, often having to

fight battalion actions to clear hilltop positions, and just as frequently suffering German counterattacks. The division was finally pulled out of the line in August 1944 for a period of rest and rehabilitation near Lake Trasimeno. Such a breather was essential, for the experience of the entire Italian campaign so far had made it abundantly clear that the Gothic Line defences would require the particular assets of the 4th Indian Division, whose capabilities in mountainous terrain were now fully appreciated.

At the end of August the US Fifth and British Eighth Armies were up against the Gothic Line defences, which stretched from the Tyrrhenian Sea to the Adriatic Sea north of Florence between La Spezia and Pesaro. Field Marshal Alexander decided on a central breakthrough by the British V Corps, secretly reinforced to seven divisions including the 4th Indian Division and the 1st Armoured Division, the latter including the 43rd Gurkha Lorried Infantry Brigade, consisting of the 2/6th,

The Gurkhas learned much from the Japanese during the Indian army's retreat through Burma in 1942, and swiftly emulated and then surpassed the Japanese in junglecraft. Here a Bren gunner of the 7th Gurkha Rifles mans a forward position in the Burma jungle, probably late in 1942.

2/8th and 2/10th Gurkha Rifles. These three battalions had been in the Middle East for some time, but the fighting for the Gothic Line was to be their first major engagement.

But before the 43rd Gurkha Brigade was available the 4th Indian Division's Gurkhas had gone into the fray, on the extreme left flank of the breakthrough area. The fighting consisted of a series of sharp attacks and counterattacks as the Gurkhas took and the Germans attempted to retake numerous hilltop towns dominating the lower regions through which the bulk of the Eighth Army had to pass. The Gurkhas were generally successful, albeit at the cost of moderate casualties, and during the first days of

By the later stages of World War II, Gurkha officers had risen to positions of relative seniority in Gurkha battalions, this order group showing Subadar Lilabur Rana, company second in command, and his three platoon commanders before an assault south of the Senio river in Italy during January 1945.

September the path was opened for V Corps by the capture of places such as Tavoleto, Auditore, Poggio San Giovanni and Passano Ridge. This last saw the debut of the 43rd Gurkha Brigade, which fought as conventional infantry in extremely difficult terrain, so broken by gullies and the like that a co-ordinated attack was impossible. Instead the Gurkhas moved in as small parties towards individual target areas, finally charging with bayonet and kukri to crush the German resistance. However, the German artillery had targeted these areas, and the victorious Gurkhas had then to withstand some 24 hours of intense bombardment.

The brigade was then switched to the 56th (London) Division for the assault crossing of the River Marecchia in late September. This operation was very nearly a disaster because of faulty intelligence: corps and army intelligence refused to accept local reports that the Germans were emplaced in strength, and so decided on an unsupported infantry

Seen during a practice jump are men of the 3/7th Gurkha Rifles, the Gurkha component of the Indian Parachute Regiment. No use was made of the regiment in its planned role during World War II, though the invasion of Malaya would have secured it employment had the war lasted that long.

Men of the 6th Gurkha Rifles wait for their armoured support to move up before sweeping forward against a Japanese position in the Singu area of Burma. Note the triple containers for mortar bombs carried by some men.

crossing, with armour and artillery support to be furnished only after a delay of 24 hours. The 43rd Brigade's Gurkhas were thus embroiled in a particularly severe action in which the Germans in their commanding positions were able to direct sustained machine-gun, mortar and artillery fire on the hapless attackers. A few tanks were able to provide some support for the Gurkhas, but it was not until well after nightfall on 23 September that the infantry was able to move up to the crest of the ridge dominating the crossing and evict the Germans, allowing a

successful conclusion to the crossing by the middle of the following day. Casualties had been heavy, especially in the 2/10th Gurkhas, but the brigade had fully confirmed the enviable standing of Gurkha infantry, behaving with exemplary skill and determination during its baptism of fire.

Farther to the east the two Gurkha battalions of the 4th Indian Division were still pressing ahead with the leading elements of the corps, but were then pulled out of the line for service in Greece just as the division was closing up to the River Rubicon.

The brunt of Gurkha operations thus fell to the 43rd Brigade, which was switched from division to division as the situation demanded the particular skills of the Gurkha battalions, which acquired a considerable reputation as river-crossing experts in the late autumn of 1944. River after river was crossed as the Germans were driven slowly back towards the valley of the River Po, which would clearly be an objective for the 1945 campaign that would terminate the war in Italy. The 43rd Brigade was finally pulled out for a rest at the end of October 1944, and after a brief spell of operations as part of the 2nd New Zealand Division for the reduction of Faenza in December 1944, sat out the winter in preparation for the 1945 spring offensive. By this time the brigade was part of the Polish II Corps, and was tasked with the vital mission of deep exploitation after major breakthroughs had been made by the planned crossings of the Senio and Santerno rivers. The offensive got under way on 9 April 1945, and the services of the 43rd Brigade were not at first needed. However, from 16 April onwards the Gurkhas proved their worth in two significant river crossings and deep exploitation thereafter in their Kangaroo armoured personnel carriers. The first crossing resulted in the capture of Medecina by the 2/6th

Gurkhas and 14/20th Hussars, and the second saw the development of a useful penetration of the German defences north of the River Gaiana. But before this latter success could be turned to further advantage the Germans in Italy surrendered on 2 May 1945.

It had been expected that when the British and Indian forces arrived in Greece at the end of 1944 they would serve as little more than garrison troops to ensure an orderly return of the democratic monarchy that had ruled the country before the German invasion of 1941. However, the guerrilla war waged against the German occupation had polarized the opposition into monarchist and communist factions, and the Allied forces soon found themselves embroiled in an embryonic civil war with potential hotspots at Salonika and Patras awaiting the outcome of events in Athens. Here communist units of the ELAS organization fought a short campaign for control of the city against British

Fort Dufferin was a key to the capture of Mandalay, and here Indian Army troops of the Fourteenth Army prepare to move forward as the gates of the fort blaze during March 1945.

units and the 5th Brigade of the 4th Indian Division.
The communists were swiftly overcome by the rapid
efforts of the British and Indians, and the Gurkha
battalions lost a few men in the process. Thereafter
the Gurkha battalions in other parts of the country
launched rapid local advances to secure the disarma-
ment of communist forces before other outbreaks of
violence could occur. The 4th Indian Division
remained in Greece until December 1945, when it
returned to India for demobilization and a return to
peacetime duties.

Thus the Gurkhas played their part and more in
the campaigns against Germany and her allies in the
west. Yet again the Gurkha infantryman had shown
himself unsurpassed in the basic skills of the
infantryman in the deserts of Iraq, the arid mountains of the Middle East, the sandy plains and dusty
mountains of the Western Desert and North Africa,
and the terrain and climatic extremes of Italy's
mountainous spine. Throughout these campaigns
the Gurkhas had achieved all that was asked of them,
winning a sincere admiration from their allies and
the very real respect of their adversaries for their
martial abilities combined with a cheerful simplicity
of nature that seemed relatively undaunted by
adversity of situation, terrain and climate.

The other arena in which the Gurkhas found
themselves in World War II was that in which the
Japanese were the enemy, ably abetted by terrain,
climate and disease. Yet again, the Gurkhas emerged
from this combination of opponents with great
distinction, and it was this theatre that saw the most
widespread use of Gurkha infantry. Yet again, space
precludes anything but a sketching of the activities
of the Gurkha Rifles, with emphasis on the regiments that eventually formed the Brigade of
Gurkhas in British service after the partition of
1947.

Given the extent of Japanese aggression on the
mainland of Asia during the 1930s, it was clear to the
British (as it was to the Dutch, French and

*Men of the 4/1st King George V's Own Gurkha Rifles
pound a Japanese position in the Sittang region of Burma
on 1 August 1945. By this time the campaign in Burma
was almost over, though the Fourteenth Army kept up the
pressure against Japanese pockets with artillery and mortar
fire wherever possible.*

One of many Gurkha recipients of the Victoria Cross was Havildar Gaje Ghale of the 5th Royal Gurkha Rifles.

Naik Agansing Rai won the Victoria Cross while serving with the 5th Royal Gurkha Rifles in the Bishenpur area of Burma during June 1944.

The Gurkhas also played a distinguished part in the Italian campaign, in the course of which Rifleman Thaman Gurung of the 5th Royal Gurkha Rifles was awarded the Victoria Cross for his gallantry at Monte San Bartolo in November 1944.

Americans) that Japan clearly had additional territorial ambitions, particularly towards South-East Asia, the Malay peninsula and the Dutch East Indies with their considerable quantities of raw materials such as rubber, oil, tin and other minerals. What was not as clear was the scope and very capability of these Japanese ambitions, backed as they were by armed forces of considerable military strength and political clout. To the British the Malay peninsula was itself a vital asset, and the fortress of Singapore at its southern extremity was the linch-pin of British communications and trade to the Far East and Australasia. Thus even in the dark days of 1940 and 1941 when the German star seemed so powerfully in the ascendant in the west, substantial forces were allocated to the defence of Malaya and Singapore. As events were to prove, these forces were neither substantial enough nor provided with the modern weapons they would need to face a wholly underestimated Japanese opponent.

Part of the garrison of Malaya was found by Gurkha battalions, including the 2/2nd Gurkha Rifles who arrived in the theatre in September 1941. The battalion was part of the 11th Indian Division, allocated to the offensive/defensive plan designed to protect the north of Malaya. As part of this scheme the 2/2nd Gurkhas were based at Alor Star in the north-west of the country, and were thus in action virtually from the moment the Japanese crossed the border from Siam, where their 5th and 18th Divisions had landed at Singora and Patani on 8 December 1941. Despite their relative lack of training for what was to emerge as the Malayan pattern of warfare, the Japanese proved themselves masterful exponents of the terrain and darkness, the 2/2nd Gurkhas first intimation that the war had reached them on 11 December coming when the Japanese had already infiltrated the 11th Indian Division's line to close in a hand-to-hand fight.

It was an inauspicious start to an ultimately disastrous campaign: the Gurkhas achieved some notable small-scale tactical successes, often blunting the speed of the Japanese advance down the west coast of Malaya towards Singapore, but the men's real problem was exhaustion as they marched south without the promised motor transport, lack of food and other supplies, and the fact that they were operating in an almost total vacuum so far as intelligence of the enemy's real positions and intentions was concerned. Action concerted with that of other units was impossible to achieve, and though the battalion remained intact, all it could achieve was its own short-term salvation rather than any real stemming of the Japanese advance, which was notable for its speed, aggression and mercurial

tactics, including small-scale but nonetheless dangerous landings in the rear of the retreating British.

The 11th Indian Division attempted to hold the line of the River Slim, but the Japanese scorned casualties and poured in a stream of armoured vehicles until the division's position was overrun. The catastrophe caught the 2/2nd Gurkhas and 2/9th Gurkhas on the wrong side of the river, and during the two battalions' efforts to regain the British lines in small parties the 2/2nd Gurkhas were reduced by half when two whole companies (and a substantial portion of the 2/9th Gurkhas) were captured. This dire day was capped by the decision of the Allied commander-in-chief, General Sir Archibald Wavell, to abandon the Malay peninsula and to concentrate his remaining assets for the defence of Singapore island, which conventional military wisdom deemed impregnable.

The decision left large portions of southern Malaya strewn with more or less disorganized pockets of Australian, British, Gurkha and Indian troops all seeking to regain the 'safety' of the island. Most of the surviving Gurkhas managed to pull back to the island by the time that the causeway linking it with the mainland was blown up on 31 January 1942. Now at last the defence began to consider the implications of a major attack from the landward side, whereas all previous assessments, plans and preparations had considered only a seaward assault. This impossible defence problem was compounded by the fact that the island's water supply had been cut by the demolition of the causeway, leaving the normal population and garrison, swollen by many thousands of refugees and retreating servicemen, to survive on the stocks of a few non-replenishable reservoirs.

The 2/2nd Gurkhas were put into the defensive line on the northern shore of the island near the Naval Base, and were soon committed to action when the Japanese during the night of 8/9 February launched a three-division invasion across the Johore Strait. The problem for the defence was exacerbated by the fact that the main Japanese assault fell on the Australians holding the western end of the line. Forced to pull back in the face of relentless Japanese attacks, the Australians failed to inform the 11th Indian Division of its intentions, so opening a large gap in the Allied line and leaving the 11th Indian Division with an exposed left flank. The division fought on grimly, the 2/2nd Gurkhas and 2/9th Gurkhas playing a notable part as the formation fell back towards the city of Singapore. But defeat was inevitable, and the survivors of the two Gurkha battalions 'went into the bag' with the surrender of Singapore on 15 February 1942. They then faced some three and a half years of dreadful incarceration before those who lived could be released.

Already, however, the Japanese had shifted the focus of their strategic attention to the west, where Burma was next in line for invasion and subjugation. Here the garrison included the 1/7th Gurkha Rifles, forward-located close to the Siamese frontier. The battalion was engaged right from the beginning of the campaign on 15 January 1942, one of its companies being destroyed in the first few hours of the invasion. Outnumbered, outgunned and generally outfought, the British-led forces were forced back from the frontier regions in a nightmare retreat in which information and orders were woefully lacking and so made the establishment of any coherent defence next to impossible. Forward defence was entrusted to the 17th Indian Division commanded by Major General Jack Smythe, and the three brigades of this formation soon included three Gurkha battalions, the 1/7th being joined by the 3/7th and 1/10th Gurkhas, as the division fell back towards the Sittang river, the last point at which the Japanese could be checked before Rangoon. But the Japanese got to the bridge over the river before the

The organic anti-tank capability of infantry units right into 1943 was provided by 6-pdr anti-tank guns such as this example in Gurkha hands near Medenine in Tunisia on 16 March 1943.

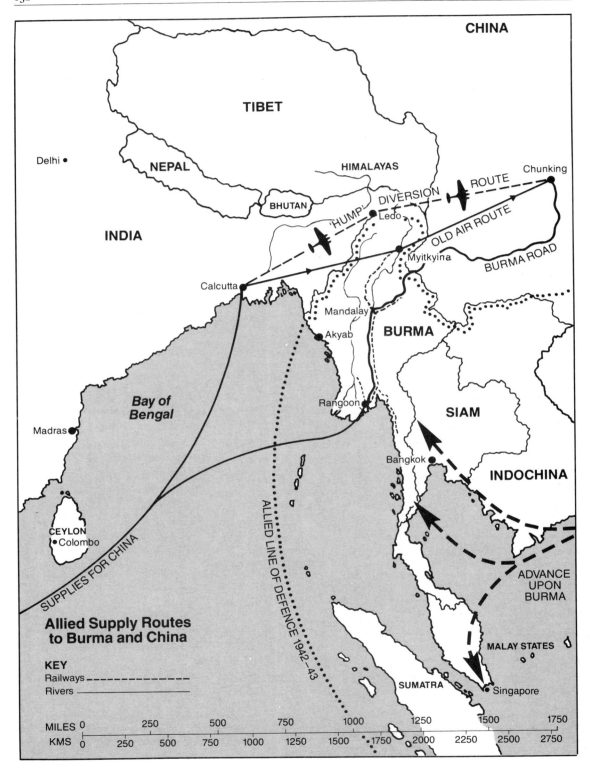

CHINA

TIBET

Delhi

NEPAL

HIMALAYAS

Chunking

BHUTAN

'HUMP' DIVERSION ROUTE

Ledo

INDIA

OLD AIR ROUTE

Myitkyina

BURMA ROAD

Calcutta

Mandalay

Akyab

BURMA

Bay of
Bengal

Rangoon

SIAM

Bangkok

INDOCHINA

Madras

SUPPLIES FOR CHINA

CEYLON
Colombo

ALLIED LINE OF DEFENCE 1942–43

ADVANCE
UPON
BURMA

**Allied Supply Routes
to Burma and China**

MALAY STATES

KEY
Railways ------------
Rivers ————————

SUMATRA

Singapore

MILES	0		250		500		750		1000		1250		1500		1750

KMS	0	250	500	750	1000	1250	1500	1750	2000	2250	2500	2750

British defence had been properly organized, and Smythe had reluctantly to order its destruction before large portions of his division had crossed. A monumental fire-fight developed during the battle for the bridge, and among the casualties of this sorry episode were the two battalions of the 7th Gurkhas, who were trapped on the wrong side of the river. Many tried to regain the western bank on rafts or by swimming, tasks made almost impossibly hard by the breadth of the river and the speed of its stream. It is believed that some 350 men were lost at this time, and the remainder of the two battalions fell into Japanese hands.

This disaster, and the impossibility of delivering substantial reinforcements to Burma, made the loss of the country inevitable. All that was left was to evacuate as many men with as much materiel as possible by the overland route to India up the major river valleys and across the mountains into Manipur and Assam. The retreat was conducted skilfully in the face of intense Japanese pressure, and must surely rank as one of the epic retreats in military history, which all too unfortunately contains many British retreats. The surviving Gurkhas played a prominent part in the withdrawal, in which the Japanese were prepared to take moderately heavy losses by infiltrating units round the flanks of the retreating British to establish and hold roadblocks to the last men. The more cumbersome British and Indian troops were generally restricted to the roads and rivers by their lack of jungle training, and the elimination of such Japanese blocks seriously delayed the retreat, giving the tired Japanese main forces ample opportunity to close up and harass the rear.

Of the Allied troops, the Gurkhas proved the most readily adaptable to the new tactics, and were often involved in the sharp actions to clear Japanese blocking positions. It is perhaps illuminating to consider one of the most successful actions fought by the Gurkhas, this time the three battalions of the 48th Brigade (1/7th, 1/4th and 2/5th Gurkhas) to check the Japanese 18th Division as it advanced on Kyaukse in the Irrawaddy valley. The brigade's defence enabled the Chinese Fifth Army to pull back in good order, and the defence was established south of the town on 27 April 1942. The Japanese closed on the town during the following day and launched a frontal attack in the evening. The Gurkhas displayed exemplary fire discipline, allowing the Japanese to close to within a mere 100 yards before opening fire. Devastated by this cohesive defence, the leading elements of the 18th Division fell back in confusion before mounting another attack a few hours later; this was handled similarly to the first, and the Japanese halted operations temporarily to reassess the situation, which was further confused by a sharp counterattack by the 1/7th Gurkhas at dawn on 29 April.

Fighting resumed during the afternoon, by which time it had become clear that the Fifth Army had withdrawn over the Ava bridge. The brigade was thus able to withdraw its battalions singly in a classic fall-back action, leaving the Japanese totally disorganized and in no fit state for rapid pursuit to the strategic Ava bridge. The British retreat continued as a race as much against time as the Japanese, and most units had reached safety just before the monsoon broke in late May 1942, halting further operations. The 17th Indian Division was now located in Imphal, where defensive preparations were instituted as the battalions of the division were brought back up to strength with fresh men and equipment, and a strenuous round of training inaugurated to teach the men the type of warfare they would clearly need in the future.

In the short term there was little chance of a British return to Burma, at least in strength, and the high command thus accepted the suggestion of Brigadier General Orde Wingate that the Japanese could be harried in Burma by specially trained and capably led long-range penetration columns, operating in the enemy's rear with the aid of air supply to cut communications and disturb Japanese rule. It was also appreciated that such operations, if successfully conducted by the specialist Chindit units, would boost Allied morale in the area by showing that the Japanese could be worsted in the tactics and terrain in which the enemy had gained an awesome but perhaps unjustified reputation.

Wingate thus trained the 77th Brigade in his new concept, and among the battalions of this brigade was the 3/2nd Gurkhas, a newly-raised battalion preferred by Wingate because its men would not be stuck in the rut of conventional tactics. The theory was fine, but the practice was not, perhaps because

Wingate steadfastly insisted on mixed units and so deprived the Gurkhas of their accustomed officers: the battalion commander was Lieutenant Colonel L.A. Alexander, and he (for example) was given command of the Southern Group, a decoy force of two columns for the Northern Group's five strike columns, designed to wreak havoc in the Japanese rear areas to facilitate the Chinese capture of the strategic town of Myitkyina. The Gurkhas were themselves divided among four columns, and as a result lost much of the identity so necessary for these Nepalese tribesmen, most of whom were also very young.

The expedition set off on 6 February 1943, and achieved only moderate successes though gaining a

A scene typical of the closing stages of the war in North Africa: Gurkha riflemen storm forward under smoke to take an Axis position in Tunisian mountain terrain on 16 March 1943.

mass of experience that was of general use to the Fourteenth Army and the second Chindit expedition. Casualties were caused by the Japanese and disease, and only about two-thirds of the committed force ever returned, most of these being totally unfit for duty in the next few months as a result of their emaciation and illnesses. The 3/2nd Gurkhas lost some 446 men, though of these 150 subsequently turned up after slow individual journeys home through the jungles and mountains of northern Burma.

It was nonetheless decided that the risks were justified by the possible benefits, and Wingate was given permission to organize a second, but much larger, expedition of divisional rather than brigade size. Wingate had learned his lesson, and this time accepted only well-established battalions whose maturity was now considered essential for deep-penetration operations. Three Gurkha battalions were allocated to Wingate's six-brigade 3rd Indian

Riflemen Sherbahadur Thapa of the 1/9th Gurkha Rifles wins the Victoria Cross for outstanding courage as he brings back a wounded comrade under heavy enemy fire.

Division: these were the 3/6th Gurkhas in the 77th Indian Brigade, and the 3/4th and 4/9th Gurkhas in the 111th Indian Brigade. None of these battalions was part of the regular establishment, but contained more experienced men than had the 3/2nd Gurkhas, and had benefited from a considerably longer period of training before the division was committed, still with the same strategic objective, on 5 March 1944. The second Chindit expedition proved more successful than the first, but again losses were heavy, and the survivors were generally incapacitated for a considerable period. The 77th Indian Brigade and its 3/6th Gurkhas particularly distinguished themselves under the command of Brigadier Michael Calvert, especially in the capture of Mogaung on 23 June 1944. Shortly after this the remnants of the brigade were evacuated by air after three months behind Japanese lines: the 3/6th Gurkhas had lost

126 dead and 350 wounded, and returned to the war only in its closing stages. Wingate had been killed in a plane crash during the second expedition, and without his charismatic effect on Allied leaders, the Chindit notion was quietly dropped.

It is worth looking more closely at the capture of Mogaung, however, for here the 3/6th Gurkhas won two Victoria Crosses. The first of these went to Captain Michael Almand for his extreme bravery in single-handedly charging a Japanese machine-gun nest although he had already been wounded and was suffering so badly from trench foot that he could hardly walk; Almand's VC was posthumous, this officer dying on 23 June of his wounds. The other VC was awarded to Rifleman Tulbahadur Pun, who was largely responsible for the capture of the Red House: although his section had been reduced to four men including himself, Tulbahadur led two men in a frontal assault which wounded Tulbahadur's two comrades, leaving the rifleman to continue alone with his Bren gun in the killing of three Japanese, the capture of two machine-guns and the routing of the other Japanese in the house. Tulbahadur survived the episode.

Meanwhile greater events had been occupying the main attention of the Fourteenth Army, namely the operations to try to recapture the Arakan region, and the Japanese attempt to break through to India after capturing Imphal and Kohima. Gurkhas had been involved in the abortive first British effort in January 1943, and in the Japanese offensive designed to oust the British in December 1943, but played a greater role in the final British success in this disease-ridden area during January 1945, when the British XV Corps drove out the Japanese Twenty-eighth Army. This oddly constituted corps comprised the 81st and 82nd West African Divisions and the 25th and 26th Indian Divisions, the 25th Division including the 3rd/2nd Gurkhas, returning to action for the first time after the battalion's revival following its tribulations in the first Chindit expedition. The battalion had reached the 25th Indian Division in the autumn of 1943, but had then spent nearly one year in acclimatizing itself to this swampy region and in completing its training before the initial moves towards the capture of Akyab were taken in September 1944.

The first move was the capture of Point 1433 by the Gurkhas, an effort greatly aided by the liberal allocation of artillery to the region, which finally caused the Japanese to withdraw though not before their stubborn defence had cost the Gurkhas some 90 casualties. However, for the Japanese the writing was now on the wall, and in January 1945 they pulled out of the northern Arakan, permitting an un-opposed advance to the vital sea port of Akyab which the 3/2nd Gurkhas were first to enter on 4 January 1945. The corps then pushed on into southern Akyab with a series of amphibious operations and overland advances, outflanking the Japanese defence lines wherever possible and forcing them cont-inuously back, so that by the end of February 1945 there was a good chance of cutting the Twenty-eighth Army's escape route from the Arakan and capturing it.

One of the keys to this region was the Snowdon Ridge, which was seized by the 3/2nd Gurkhas without a shot fired on 4 March. However, the Japanese then decided to retake the ridge, and a small but bloody battle raged before the Gurkhas

were left in decisive control after losing one-third of their men dead and wounded. The action also brought a Victoria Cross to Rifleman Bhanbhagta Gurung for his decisive part in the recapture of Snowdon East. Bhanbhagta's company had five times been pinned down by Japanese machine-gun fire, and five times led forward by Bhanbagta's charges. Bhanbhagta was first into the Japanese defensive position, where he killed the surviving Japanese with his kukri, and then organized an impromptu defence that crushed a despairing Japanese counterattack. This closed the Twenty-eighth Army's escape route to southern Burma, and though the monsoon prevented further operations, the Twenty-eighth Army was thus prevented from regaining the main Japanese forces in Burma in the closing stages of the war, being forced to sit it out in ghastly conditions of disease and starvation before surrendering in August 1945.

The end of 1943 was also notable for the beginning of the Japanese campaign designed to take Imphal and Kohima and so open the way into India. Throughout the summer the British and Japanese forces had watched intently as each side prepared for the inevitable confrontation, and by October both sides had been considerably reinforced, to the extent that the Japanese started a series of probing raids and diversionary attacks designed to evaluate the British defences while securing the optimum jumping-off points for the offensive, scheduled to begin in March 1944. In these small-scale but nonetheless important moves the Gurkhas of the 17th, 20th and 23rd Indian Divisions played a distinguished part, rapidly gaining the experience and will to tackle the Japanese in the jungle that had previously been one of the latter's main 'friends'. The progress of such operations also proved of invaluable assistance in developing the tactical skills of wartime Gurkha battalions, who had hitherto lacked the combat experience of their regular bro-thers, and the fear of Gurkha raids began to play a decided morale-sapping part in the decline of Japanese capabilities.

The Imphal/Kohima area was the responsibility of IV Corps within the Fourteenth Army, and in all the corps could call on the services of 11 Gurkha battalions, as part of its three organic divisions, others being added later by the addition of the 153rd

The theatre in which the Gurkhas played their most decisive part in World War II was Burma, where the Gurkhas were a mainstay of the Fourteenth Army. And within this theatre one of the Gurkhas' most distinguished services was in the defence of Imphal. Seen here are men of the 3/10th Gurkha Rifles after their success in the battle for Scraggy, the smoke-shrouded feature in the background being Scraggy Pimple.

Gurkha Parachute Battalion of the 50th Indian Parachute Brigade.

First indications of the Japanese advance were not long in arriving, though the scale and speed of the movement were a nasty surprise for the Fourteenth Army command. It was decided, therefore, to pull back the outlying divisions and concentrate the strength of IV Corps at Imphal. This sudden withdrawal was not appreciated by the Gurkhas in particular, for they had been taking the war most decidedly to the Japanese, and given their lack of

high command information saw little reason to fall back. Nevertheless it was the right move, and while the three divisions of IV Corps allowed themselves to be pushed back to Imphal by the Japanese 15th and 33rd Divisions the 161st Brigade of the XXXIII Corps was to hold Kohima against the Japanese 31st Division. General Slim remained confident that the Japanese were overextending themselves, and that the forces holding the two bastions could with air support and supply withstand the Japanese siege while major counteroffensive forces were prepared for the relief of the garrisons and then the pursuit of the broken Japanese divisions. And so it turned out, though the sieges of Imphal and Kohima proved far more dangerous than had been anticipated. Kohima was cut off on 4 April and Imphal on 5 April 1944, and the eventual relief of the garrisons followed only on 18 April and 22 June 1944 respectively. The desperation of the fighting in the steep hills of

Manipur is well known, and it suffices to say that the fighting in and around the Imphal area saw the Gurkhas in magnificent form, the men being right in their element in the close-quarter fighting that marked much of the battle. Artillery and armour also played their part in the operations, the latter offering Rifleman Ganju Lama of the 1/7th Gurkhas the chance to win his Victoria Cross.

This stirring episode occurred on 12 June, when the 2/5th Gurkhas holding Ningthoukhong were hard pressed to cope with a Japanese armoured attack. Reinforcements, comprising two companies of the 1/7th Gurkhas, were sent up to help. However, the reinforcements were caught by a trio of Japanese tanks and pinned down. Ganju was something of a specialist in tank destruction, though, for he had already won the Military Medal for taking out two Japanese tanks in a previous operation. Wriggling forward to engage these three, Ganju was severely wounded in the arms and legs (his left wrist being smashed) but succeeded in knocking out the two leading tanks and killing their crews. Just as the second tank was destroyed, the last machine was hit by an anti-tank projectile and knocked out, but as its crew scrambled out Ganju hurled grenades at them, killing the entire crew. It is an indication of the severity of the fighting, and of the part played in it by the Gurkhas, that this was only one of five Gurkha VCs won in that month: those of Captain M. Almand and Rifleman Tulbahadur Pun have already been mentioned, and the other two went to Rifleman Agansing Rai and to Acting Subedar Netrabahadur Thaps, both of the 2nd/5th Royal Gurkha Rifles for their gallantry in the attack on a Japanese roadblock in the Ningthoukhong which took nearly seven days of intense fighting and cost the battalion some 176 casualties. But by the end of June the Japanese had shot their bolt and began to pull back, having lost as battle casualties or disease victims some 75,000 of the 100,000 men who had launched Operation 'U-GO'. Nevertheless the Japanese Fifteenth Army remained a cohesive unit as it pulled back to the line of the Chindwin river, despite the attentions of the Fourteenth Army and its ever-strengthening air support in hot pursuit.

Along the Chindwin matters slowed for some months as the exhausted opponents regathered their strength and the British prepared to strike across the Chindwin in November with the objective of taking the key cities of Mandalay and Meiktila, whose loss could cut off the Japanese Fifteenth and Thirty-third Armies in the north of Burma. The attack on Mandalay was the responsibility of XXXIII Corps' British 2nd and Indian 19th and 20th Divisions, while the capture of Meiktila was the responsibility of IV Corps' 17th Indian Division. Mandalay was taken on 20 March 1945, some 17 days after the fall of Meiktila. Both advances by the British and Indians had been accomplished only at the expense of strenuous fighting, but so far as the Gurkhas were concerned undoubtedly the most important actions were those at Meiktila and Kyaukmyaung. Meiktila was captured by the 17th Indian Division and its several Gurkha battalions with little difficulty on 3 March, but was then encircled by the Japanese who had belatedly realized the strategic importance of Meiktila's loss to themselves. Bitter fighting raged in the city until 29 March, when the beleaguered 17th Indian Division was at last able to make contact with forces advancing from Mandalay, whose defences had been seriously weakened as General Kimura, commanding the Burma Area Army, brought in units from three Japanese divisions in a last-ditch effort to wrest back control of the city. Thus Meiktila and its defence by the 17th Indian Division greatly aided the advance of XXXIII to Mandalay, as well as closing the main artery by which the defeated Japanese could have fled south. No greater an item of praise could have been released about the 17th Indian Division's holding of Meiktila than the later comment of Kimura that it was the 'master stroke of the whole campaign in Burma'.

Kyaukmyaung was the site of another magnificent performance by an Indian division with a substantial number of Gurkhas. This time it was the 19th Indian Division, which secured a bridgehead on the eastern bank of the Irrawaddy on 11 January 1945 and thereafter held this against fanatically determined counterattacks for some five weeks until the division broke out to the south and Mandalay, again after drawing off substantial numbers of Japanese defenders from Mandalay proper.

The loss of Meiktila and Mandalay marked the effective end of Japanese resistance in Burma. Thereafter there developed a race down the Sittang and Irrawaddy rivers as British and Indian divisions raced south against some Japanese resistance and the threat of the monsoon, whose arrival before the capture of Rangoon could leave the Fourteenth Army camped in the Burmese plains at the end of hopelessly long lines of communication with India. The race was won by the Allies, for on 1 May 1945 the men of the Gurkha Parachute Battalion landed on the east side of the Irrawaddy estuary and marched unopposed into Rangoon on 3 May before advancing to meet the advance guard of the 17th Indian Division moving south down the Sittang valley at Hlegu on 6 May. The Japanese were now firmly trapped in Burma, and though they made a desperate attempt to break out towards Siam in July, the 17th and 19th Indian Divisions were waiting for such a move and slaughtered the Japanese in their emaciated thousands. Yet the Japanese refused to capitulate until the end of World War II in August.

The sudden collapse of the Japanese caught the Allies generally unprepared for the outbreak of peace, but troops were soon landed in Malaya, where one of the more pleasant tasks was the liberation of many thousands of prisoners of war after their terrible time in Japanese hands. Parties of troops were soon despatched all over the country on policing duties and to round up groups of lost Japanese, though the high command had additional tasks in hand as the French and Dutch were not yet ready to assume control of their erstwhile colonies without British and Indian military support. Thus the Gurkhas found themselves in Indo-China and the Dutch East Indies, and once again into the thick of two shooting wars. In Indo-China the 20th Indian Division with the 4/2nd Gurkhas and 4/10th Gurkhas faced the problem of maintaining order in a situation in which the returning French were opposed militarily and politically by a nationalist movement that had grown strong during a resistance war against the occupying Japanese. Indeed, so tense

was the position and so few the numbers of trained troops to oppose the nationalists that the general commanding the 20th Indian Division had to enlist the services of Japanese prisoners of war. However, after a month of fairly open fighting with the nationalists, the 20th Indian Division was able to depart from Saigon as the French claimed to have matters under control.

The situation was more involved still in Java, where in many instances the Japanese had surrendered to the Indonesian nationalists, who had taken over local prisoner of war camps to hold their occupants hostage against the returning Dutch. Into this imbroglio arrived the 23rd Indian Division with the 3/10th Gurkhas. Realizing the dangers of the situation, the local Japanese commander halted the surrender of his men and set about retaking the prisoner of war camps. The 23rd Indian Division landed on 19 October to find the Japanese in partial control. Trouble with the nationalists inevitably erupted, and again the division was forced to use Japanese troops alongside its own. The division remained in Java for one year, and was involved in a number of serious incidents and actions as the Dutch fought to regain control of the East Indies.

Finally all the Gurkha battalions had returned home and started the process of demobilization that would return their establishment to the pre-war norm. But the India to which the Gurkhas had returned was not the same India in which they had trained and for which they had fought: nationalism was now a force of immense divisive strength, and in many instances returning troops were treated almost as pariahs in circumstances where returning men of the Indian National Army that had fought for the Japanese were treated as heroes. The end of British rule in the Indian subcontinent was well in sight, and with it a total reassessment of the Gurkhas' place in the Indian military establishment.

The long voyage from the UK to the Falklands during 1982 presented problems in keeping the men fit and tuned for action, and the former at least was eased by the size of the troopships, the men of the 7th Gurkhas travelling on the liner Queen Elizabeth 2 *with all her modern facilities.*

PARTITION
AND AFTER

By 1946 the Indian army felt able to begin the demobilization of Gurkha battalions, and by the decisive year of 1947 all the war-raised fourth battalions, with the exception of the 4/2nd Gurkhas, had been disbanded while the three fifth battalions had been re-formed as the lost battalions of their regiments. The situation with the third battalions was more complex: those of the 7th and 10th Gurkhas had been disbanded, that of the 2nd Gurkhas had been combined with the second battalion, and the others remained in being.

This reduction in basic strength was accompanied by the first moves towards a fundamental reorganization of the Gurkha units in total, for the partition of British India into the dominions of India and Pakistan had been agreed in 1947 and with this move came the need to decide the future of the Gurkha regiments. Not surprisingly, rumours abounded and a considerable degree of anxiety was felt by the Gurkha and British personnel alike of the surviving battalions before the future was decided; the Gurkha regiments were to be maintained in being, but divided between the British and Indian armies. Complex negotiations between the British, Indian and Nepalese governments confirmed that four of the Gurkha regiments would fall to the British army and that the other six would remain part of the Indian army. The regiments designated to become

Right: Men of the 7th Gurkhas pose with a Rheinmetall Rh 202 twin 20-mm anti-aircraft cannon system captured from the Argentines in the Falklands War.

Bottom right: The 7th Duke of Edinburgh's Own Gurkha Rifles served with great distinction in the Falklands War of 1982 alongside British units, and are here epitomized by a quartet of riflemen applying camouflage before being flown into combat by helicopter.

Below: Men of the 7th Duke of Edinburgh's Own Gurkha Rifles collect an illegal immigrant during border patrol in Hong Kong.

Pictured after his promotion to sergeant, Rambahadur Limbu was serving as a lance-corporal in The 10th Princess Mary's Own Gurkha Rifles when he became the most recent Gurkha winner of the Victoria Cross for his gallantry in November 1965 within the context of the 'Indonesian Confrontation'.

Although it is unimpressive so far as its present temporary quarters are concerned, the Gurkha Museum at Church Crookham has very many fascinating exhibits and a most hospitable and informative staff.

As well as patrolling on foot along Hong Kong's land frontier with China, the present Gurkha garrison co-operates with the civil forces in the prevention of illegal immigration by sea. Here, a boat patrol prepares to investigate a junk suspected of carrying illegal immigrants.

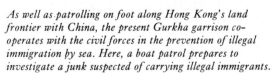

Lance-Corporal Jock Goughlin and Corporal Narsing Pun, Gurkha Military Police, patrol in search of communist terrorists in 1957 as part of British operations during the Malayan Emergency. Goughlin is armed with a 0.303-in Rifle No. 5 while Narsing carries an American weapon, the 0.3-in Carbine M1.

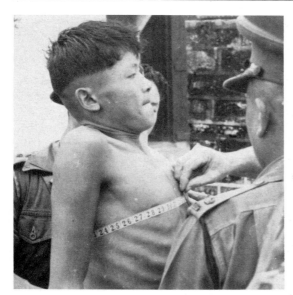

A Gurkha recruit does his best to impress during a physical examination in about 1950. For each vacancy, the depots in Nepal accept two young men for final selection, the recruiting officers having assessed perhaps as many as 300 potential recruits for each vacancy. Recruitment is generally regional: the 2nd Goorkhas and 6th Gurkhas recruit in the west of Nepal among the Magars and Gurungs, the 7th and 10th Gurkhas in the east among the Limbus and Rais, and the engineer, signal and transport regiments from both groupings.

Flanked by two Queen's Gurkha Orderly Officers at a Buckingham Palace reception in 1956 are six legendary Victoria Cross holders of the Brigade of Gurkhas. From left to right these are WO(1) Tulbahadur Pun of the 6th Gurkha Rifles, Subadar Major Gaje Ghale of the 5th Royal Gurkha Rifles, Major (QGO) Lalbahadur Thapa of the 2nd Goorkha Rifles, Subadar Major Ganju Lama of the 7th Gurkha Rifles, Havildar Bhanbhakta Gurung of the 3/2nd Goorkha Rifles and Subadar Agansing Rai of the 5th Royal Gurkha Rifles.

part of the British army were the 2nd Gurkha Rifles, the 6th Gurkha Rifles, the 7th Gurkha Rifles and the 10th Gurkha Rifles, from 1 January 1948 designated the Brigade of Gurkhas.

Once the decision had been made, the Indian army moved with considerable speed to declare its intentions for the Gurkhas in terms of pay, conditions of service, retirement allocation and pension rights, while the British army was far more dilatory. The result was that when the men of the four regiments allocated to the British army were offered the choice of remaining with their own battalion, or of transferring to an Indian battalion, or of discharge with compensation, many opted for the latter two courses. Three factors militated for this relatively large-scale decision to opt out of British service: first was the dilatory nature of the British decision on terms of service; second was the fact that a decision for British service would mean a completely different way of life, with service based far from Nepal rather than just over the border; and third was the pressure, both deliberate and unconscious, exerted by a number of Viceroy Commissioned Officers and NCOs, who in proportionally greater numbers decided for Indian service and tried to take their men with them. Each Gurkha was given a wholly free choice in the matter, the answer being given to a tribunal of one British, one Indian and one Nepalese representative, but the decision of many VCOs and NCOs to shift to the Indian army undoubtedly influenced many of the riflemen to make a similar decision.

Thus, when the eight battalions of the 2nd, 6th, 7th and 10th Gurkhas quit India for their new homes in Malaya at the beginning of 1948, both morale and numbers were on the low side. Particularly important was the loss of many experienced VCOs and NCOs, and the dearth of specialists such as signallers, drivers and administrative staff. It is indicative of the basic strength of the Gurkha regiments, however, that recruitment quickly brought numbers back to establishment during the initial months of the year. Training assumed an even more vital aspect as these recruits were integrated into battalions that were finding their feet in a completely different milieu. Traditions and ceremonial were lovingly cherished wherever possible as a means of continuing a way of life, but the removal of the battalions from their 'homes' had a profound effect, slowly overcome by the tireless efforts of dedicated British officers and their Queen's Gurkha Officer (QVO) companions.

In India the Gurkhas' lives remained much as before, though changes had inevitably to be made to accommodate the battalions to life under Indian rather than British officers. Another modification to the Gurkhas' way of life was inevitable after the partition, for the previous base at Abbottabad was allotted to the fledgling Pakistan army. Within the Indian army, therefore, the surviving regiments were grouped with the 1st and 4th Gurkhas at the regimental centre in Sabathu (the previous stations of Dharamsala and Bakloh being abandoned), the

Though obviously posed, this illustration of riflemen of the 7th Gurkhas reveals the uniform pattern and size of the modern kukri, which is still an excellent close-quarter personal weapon of distinctive shape and lethal capabilities.

A rifleman of the 2nd Goorkhas shows off the rakish angle at which the standard bush hat is worn by the Gurkha regiments.

3rd and 9th Gurkhas at the regimental centre at Dehra Dun which had been the original base of the 9th (the 3rd Gurkhas' lines at Almora and Lansdowne were forsaken in 1939), and the 5th and 8th Gurkhas at the regimental centre in Dehra Dun

previously the home of the 2nd Gurkhas. A new 11th Gurkhas was raised by the Indian army, and home for this regiment is the erstwhile base of the 3rd Gurkhas. The tradition and way of life of the Gurkhas has since thrived with the new Indian army, expansion rapidly taking the total of Gurkha

Well-kitted Gurkhas practise their skills on the boarding net of an assault course at their Hong Kong depot.

A regular round of intensive training helps to maintain the skills of the individual Gurkha, while overseas postings and larger-scale exercises provide an impetus to unit cohesion and battalion efficiency.

An intense will to excel has helped the Gurkhas to maintain their reputation as some of the world's finest infantrymen under all climatic and operational conditions.

Being lighter than the L1A1, the M16A1 automatic rifle is perhaps better suited to the relatively light physique of the average Gurkha, and there can be little doubt of the determination of this Gurkha rifleman in training at Hong Kong.

Gurkha infantrymen train in Hong Kong's New Territories. The return of the colony to China in 1997 raises the problem of what the British government will do with the Brigade of Gurkhas.

battalions to a maximum of 35, which have seen extensive and valuable service with the Indian army in several wars, notably the clashes in Kashmir, the China War of 1962, the Congo War of 1961–2 as part of the United Nations' force, and the Indo–Pakistan Wars of 1965 and 1971. The war with China proved something of a disaster for Indian arms, though the Gurkhas were a notable exception, and when between 1962 and 1965 an intensive campaign was instituted to remedy the defects made so abundantly clear in this short war, the Gurkhas were much boosted in strength and esteem. India remains highly secretive about her armed forces, and it is therefore almost impossible to expand further on the activities of the Gurkha battalions in Indian service.

The Brigade of Gurkhas in British service and stationed in Malaya during the late 1940s was designed as the precursor of a proposed Gurkha division, the 17th 'Black Cat' Gurkha Division so designated in honour of that formidable division in the Burma campaign during World War II. To perpetuate the tradition further, the three brigades of the new division were given the numbers 48, 63 and 99 as borne by the brigades of the original 17th Indian Division. Another link with the past was retained in the allocation of a crossed kukri emblem to the division, in addition to the black cat: these crossed kukris had signified another distinguished Gurkha brigade in World War II, namely the 43rd Gurkha Lorried Infantry Brigade that had seen extensive and highly successful service during the Italian campaign. As part of this expansion to divisional strength (a manpower total of some 14,000 being planned), the Gurkhas were diversified somewhat, and additional units were raised to complete the establishment of the division. Thus in 1948 a number of new units began to appear. The 7th Gurkhas for a time became the 101st and 102nd

Led by a drum-major of the 7th Gurkhas, this pipe band is found by men of the 7th Duke of Edinburgh's Own Gurkha Rifles and of The Gurkha Transport Regiment. The Scottish association of the 7th Gurkhas is confirmed by the fact that the affiliated regiment is The Queen's Own Highlanders.

Field Regiments, Royal Artillery (7th Gurkha Rifles) to provide the division's organic artillery component before reverting quite soon to its original infantry designation and role. Other units raised from 1948 were 67 Engineer Field Squadron, Royal Engineers, followed in 1950 by 68 Engineer Field Squadron, Royal Engineers, and the Gurkha Independent Signal Squadron. The engineer squadrons came under the control of a new 50th Field Engineer Regiment in 1950, and in 1958 this became an integral part of the Brigade of Gurkhas, changing its title to The Gurkha Engineers in 1960. The Gurkha Independent Signal Squadron was rapidly expanded after its formation, reflecting the increased significance of such procedures, and was in 1954

redesignated The Gurkha Signals.

Transport is also an important factor, and in 1958 two companies of the Gurkha Army Service Corps were formed in Malaya. In 1965 these were redesignated the Gurkha Transport Regiment. Provost duties were the responsibility of the Gurkha Military Police, raised in 1955, while the guarding of installations was allocated to 5 Gurkha Dog Company, itself raised in 1963. In 1966 the two police units were amalgamated as 5 Gurkha Dog Company, but this was later disbanded. And finally components of the 7th and 10th Gurkhas were trained as paratroopers from 1961 onwards, these forming the strength of The Gurkha Independent Parachute Company when it was officially formed in 1962. In 1977 The Gurkha Engineers and The Gurkha Signals were each allocated the prefix Royal as part of the honours awarded in the jubilee year of Queen Elizabeth II's reign.

The basic infantry regiments had also altered somewhat in this period: in 1959 the 6th Gurkhas

became the 6th Queen Elizabeth's Own Gurkha Rifles, in the same year the 7th Gurkhas became the 7th Duke of Edinburgh's Own Gurkha Rifles, and in 1949 the 10th Gurkhas had become the 10th Princess Mary's Own Gurkha Rifles.

The post-war period has not been one of peace for the men of the Gurkha regiments in British service, for they have been involved in a succession of relatively small but nonetheless intensive campaigns since that time, adding to their laurels and confirming their position as some of the world's best infantry. The first region to require the services of Gurkha infantry was Malaya, where in 1948 communist forces began a campaign of terrorism designed to break up the newly formed Malaysian Federation and make possible the emergence of a communist state in the region. Since that time the Gurkhas saw action in the subsequent Malayan Emergency, the Indonesian Confrontation, various troubles in Borneo and Brunei, the Cypriot war of the 1960s and Britain's war with Argentina during

Though Western music is naturally alien to them, the Gurkhas have produced excellent regimental bands notable for their smart turn-out and drill, and fully up to the musical standard of British regiments. This is the band of the 2nd Goorkha Rifles.

1982 for the Falkland Islands. The small compass of this volume precludes any detailed discussion of these activities other than a brief description of the various regiments' commitments.

The 2nd King Edward VII's Own Gurkhas (The Sirmoor Rifles) was soon committed to the Malayan Emergency in 1948, and continued in service in this dire task for the next 12 years. Casualties were relatively light, though the nature of the terrain meant that many men were injured and fell sick in the thick jungles into which the communist guerrillas were soon forced. The war was one of small-scale patrol, ambush and clever use of intelligence work, and proved admirably suited to the capabilities of the Gurkhas, whose prowess in jungle conditions had become evident during the Burma campaign in

World War II. Moreover, the individuality of the Gurkhas proved a great asset in such operations, where small patrols were often left to their own devices for considerable periods. Air resupply was an important factor, as was the air evacuation of casualties, but such jungle operations proved invaluable in proving the capability and initiative of junior commanders and NCOs under the most trying of conditions.

And a mere two years after the formal end of the Malayan Emergency, the 2nd Gurkhas were again in action, this time flying out at six hours' notice from Malaya to control a rebellion in Brunei during 1962. Further activity in this inhospitable terrain followed between 1963 and 1966 in the Indonesian Confrontation, when Indonesia attempted to capitalize upon the region's instability to assert its territorial ambitions. Prompt and unwavering response by the British government prevented any real Indonesian successes, but again the 2nd Gurkhas were with other Gurkha battalions faced with the prospect of

years in the jungles, swamps and mountains in Borneo, as groups of Indonesian regulars were rounded up after crossing into British territory. Since the termination of the Indonesian Confrontation the 2nd Gurkhas were the only Gurkha regiment to be maintained on a two-battalion basis as the Brigade of Gurkhas was reduced to five battalions in keeping with the British policy of gradual withdrawal from the Far East. This has meant the reduction of overall Gurkha strength in the British army from 14,000 to 7000 men, and as

On a training exercise in Papua New Guinea, a Gurkha rifleman reveals part of the kukri's overall utility, for the kukri is not just a fighting knife but a multi-purpose tool of great practicality in underdeveloped areas.

Local colour does little to detract from the purposeful nature of this Gurkha patrol during an exercise in Papua New Guinea. Though they originate in a high country, the Gurkhas have proved themselves adept campaigners in low, hot and humid conditions such as those in Borneo and Burma.

part of this continuing presence, the 2nd Gurkhas have since served in Brunei, Singapore, Hong Kong and in Britain.

Another Gurkha regiment to serve without relief right through the Malayan Emergency was the 6th Gurkha Rifles, in the process becoming the 6th Queen Elizabeth's Own Gurkha Rifles. Again the regiment proved the capabilities of the Gurkha as a potent instrument of jungle fighting, the regiment suffering a number of casualties during the 12-year emergency but playing a key part in the containment of the guerrillas' aspirations in Malaya, the gradual whittling away of their strength and the final relegation of surviving communist bands to a small and totally inhospitable region up against the Thai border where they finally surrendered to bring to a close the emergency. Thereafter the 1/6th Gurkhas moved to Britain as one of the first Gurkha battalions to be stationed in that country (as part of the strategic reserve), but in 1964 both battalions were committed to the Indonesian Confrontation in Borneo. The 2/6th Gurkhas served for four years in Borneo during the confrontation, longer than any other unit involved, and again proved itself adept in the specialized techniques needed for this type of warfare. The cutback in British strength in the Far East after the end of the confrontation in 1966 saw the amalgamation of the 6th Gurkhas' two battalions, and since that time the regiment has served in Brunei, the UK, Hong Kong and Belize.

The 7th Gurkha Rifles were in the process of conversion to field artillery regiments as the organic artillery of the 17th Gurkha Division when the Malayan Emergency erupted. It was soon apparent that the particular requirements of this war were for infantry rather than artillery, and the conversion process was reversed. Both battalions of the regiment served through most of the emergency, each missing only two years for a tour of guard duty in Hong Kong. The capabilities of the Gurkhas are attested by the success of the regiment: for the loss of 39 men, the 7th Gurkhas accounted for 472 guerrillas. And soon after the end of the emergency the two battalions of the 7th Gurkhas were moved into Borneo as part of the British force to crush the uprising in Brunei. The battalions stayed on in the island for the Indonesian Confrontation, in which they performed nine tours and confirmed themselves particularly skilful exponents of jungle warfare. After service in Borneo the battalions were shifted to Hong Kong, seeing unpleasant service in the border riots of 1967 and 1968. The battalions were amalgamated in August 1970 as part of the British rundown in the Far East. In 1959 the regiment had been renamed the 7th Duke of Edinburgh's Own Gurkha Rifles, and after the amalgamation of 1970 moved to Britain in 1971 for a two-year tour of duty before returning to garrison duties in Brunei and Hong Kong. A year particularly notable for the regiment was 1982, when it served with considerable distinction as part of the British forces involved in the recapture of the Falkland Islands after their illegal seizure by the Argentines, and when it was also returned to a two-battalion establishment as a second battalion was raised in Hong Kong as part of the Conservative government's reappraisal and expansion of the British armed forces.

As had the other three Gurkha regiments, the 10th Princess Mary's Own Gurkha Rifles were soon embroiled in the Malayan Emergency that started in 1948. Both battalions were involved for the full 12 years of the war, and then moved to Borneo between 1963 and 1966 for the Indonesian Confrontation.

Equipped to full British army standards, the Gurkhas are now based in Hong Kong, and, as part of their normal garrison duties, undertake patrols along the frontier of the New Territories with China. Towards the rear of this closed-up patrol is the section machine-gunner with his belt-fed 7.62-mm L7A1 general-purpose machine-gun.

A key to patrolling in forest and jungle areas is the breaking up of hard outlines, a task at which the Gurkhas are particularly adept, as illustrated by this border patrol in Hong Kong. Third from the front is a rifleman armed with a US-supplied 5.56-mm M16A1 automatic rifle, the other riflemen being equipped with the standard British 7.62-mm L1A1 semi-automatic rifle.

Engineer units make possible the movement and supply of all army units, and the Gurkhas have their own specialist engineer unit, The Queen's Gurkha Engineers, seen here road building in the New Territories. As well as honing techniques, such peacetime activities aid the civil administration and provide a wartime transport infrastructure.

Here the regiment performed with particular excellence, and secured its first Victoria Cross (and indeed the first to be won since the Korean War). The recipient was Lance-Corporal Rambahadur Limbu, for his actions during a border clash on 21 November 1965. Here the Indonesians had occupied an excellent hilltop position that could be reached only along a sharp ridge. However, a party of Gurkhas managed with very considerable skill to close in undetected to a point no more than 20 yards from the Indonesians before they were detected and engaged by a machine-gun, which wounded one of Rambahadur's men. Rambahadur immediately charged the machine-gunner and killed him, though additional Indonesian fire was now directed at the Gurkha party, which suffered another two wounded. Rambahadur then shifted his men to a less exposed position and took stock of the situation, including how best he might rescue the wounded men. In a series of short dashes Rambahadur managed to reach and bring back one of the wounded before the Indonesians were fully aware of what was happening, but then faced a more difficult task in bringing back the second man. However, the NCO finally managed to reach his comrade and drag him back to safety, and this excellent piece of leadership and courage was fully rewarded by the award of a VC.

After the end of the confrontation the regiment was shifted to Hong Kong, where it played a part in the suppression of the border problems of 1967 and 1968. Thereafter the rundown of British Far Eastern forces was upon the regiment, and in 1968 the two battalions were amalgamated in Penang. Since that time the regiment has served in Britain (being assigned for an eight-month period of emergency duty in Cyprus in 1974 at the time of the Turkish invasion), and then in Hong Kong and Brunei before returning for additional service in the United Kingdom.

Current Gurkha strength in the British army is six infantry battalions, The Queen's Gurkha Engineers, The Queen's Gurkha Signals and The Gurkha Transport Regiment. The normal basing of these assets is Hong Kong, where four battalions and support elements are based. A fifth battalion is located in the UK, and the sixth battalion is currently in Belize. There has been some doubt expressed about the future of the Brigade of Gurkhas once its base in Hong Kong is lost when the colony is returned to China in 1997, but it is probable that considerable pressure could be exerted on the government to prevent the dissolution of this excellent brigade, the legacy of nearly one and three-quarter centuries of devoted service by Nepalese soldiers.

APPENDIX I

Gurkha VCs

Name	Regiment	Place of action	Date of action	Gazetted in London Gazette
Lt J.A. Tytler	Bengal Staff Corps, serving with 66th Bengal Native Infantry	Indian Mutiny	10 February 1858	23 August 1858
Maj. D. MacIntyre	Bengal Staff Corps, serving with 2nd GR	Lushai Campaign	4 January 1872	27 September 1872
Br. Maj. G.N. Channer	Bengal Staff Corps, serving with 1st GR	Malaya	20 December 1875	12 April 1876
Capt. J. Cook	Bengal Staff Corps, serving with 5th GR	Afghanistan	2 December 1878	18 March 1879
Capt. R.K. Ridgeway	Bengal Staff Corps, serving with 44th GR	Naga Campaign	22 November 1879	11 May 1880
Lt C.J.W. Grant	Indian Staff Corps, serving with 12th Burma Regt	Manipur	27 March 1891	26 May 1891
Lt G.H. Boisragon	5th GR	Hunza Campaign	2 December 1891	12 July 1892
Lt J. Manners-Smith	Indian Staff Corps, serving with 5th GR	Hunza Campaign	20 December 1891	12 July 1892
Capt. W.G. Walker	1/4th GR	Somaliland	22 April 1903	7 August 1903
Lt J.D. Grant	1/8th GR	Tibet	6 July 1904	24 January 1905
Rfm Kulbir Thapa	2/3rd GR	France	25 September 1915	18 November 1915
Maj. G.C. Wheeler	2/9th GR	Mesopotamia	23 February 1917	8 June 1917
Rfm Karnabahadur Rana	2/3rd GR	Egypt	10 April 1918	21 June 1918
Subadar Lalbahadur Thapa	1/2nd GR	Tunisia	5/6 April 1943	15 June 1943
Havildar Gaje Ghale	2/5th RGR	Burma	24–7 May 1944	30 September 1944
A/Capt. M. Allmand	IAC attached to 6th GR	Burma	11–23 June 1944	26 October 1944
Rfm Ganju Lama	1/7th GR	Burma	12 June 1944	7 September 1944
Rfm Tulbahadur Pun	3/6th GR	Burma	23 June 1944	9 November 1944
Rfm Agansing Rai	5th RGR	Burma	24–5 June 1944	5 October 1944
A/Subadar Netrabahadur Thapa	2/5th RGR	Burma	25–6 June 1944	12 October 1944
T/Maj. F.G. Blaker	HLI attached to 3/9th GR	Burma	9 July 1944	26 September 1944
Rfm Sherbahadur Thapa	1/9th GR	Italy	18 September 1944	28 December 1944
Rfm Thaman Gurung	1/5th RGR	Italy	19 November 1944	22 February 1945
Rfm Bhanbagta Gurung	3/2nd GR	Burma	5 March 1945	5 June 1945
Rfm Lachhiman Gurung	4/8th GR	Burma	12 May 1945	27 July 1945
L/C Rambahadur Limbu	2/10th GR	Borneo	21 November 1965	22 April 1966

APPENDIX II

Title changes of Gurkha regiments

1st King George V's Own Gurkha Rifles (the Malaun Regiment)

1815 1st Nasiri Battalion
1823 5th, 6th, or 1st Nasiri Local Battalion
1826 4th, or Nasiri Local Battalion
1843 4th or Nasiri (Rifle Battalion)
1850 66th or Goorkha Regiment, Bengal Native Infantry
1858 66th or Goorkha Light Infantry Regiment, Bengal Native Infantry
1861 11th Regiment of Bengal Native Infantry
1861 1st Goorkha Regiment (Light Infantry)
1886 1st Goorkha Regiment (Light Infantry)
1891 1st Gurkha (Rifle) Regiment
1901 1st Gurkha Rifles
1903 1st Gurkha Rifles (the Malaun Regiment)
1906 1st Prince of Wales Own Gurkha Rifles
1910 1st King George's Own Gurkha Rifles (The Malaun Regiment)
1937 1st King George V's Own Gurkha Rifles (the Malaun Regiment)
1947 to Indian Army

2nd King Edward VII's Own Goorkhas (the Sirmoor Rifles)

1815 Sirmoor Battalion
1823 8th (or Sirmoor) Local Battalion
1826 6th (or Sirmoor) Local Battalion
1850 Sirmoor Battalion
1858 Sirmoor Rifle Regiment
1861 17th Regiment of Bengal Native Infantry
1861 2nd Goorkha Regiment
1864 2nd Goorkha (the Sirmoor Rifles) Regiment
1876 2nd (Prince of Wales's Own) Goorkha Regiment (the Sirmoor Rifles)
1886 2nd (the Prince of Wales's Own) Goorkha Regiment (The Sirmoor Rifles)
1891 2nd (the Prince of Wales's own) Gurkha (Rifles) Regiment (the Sirmoor Rifles)
1901 2nd (the Prince of Wales's Own) Gurkha Rifles (the Sirmoor Rifles)
1 Jan. 1906 2nd King Edward's Own Gurkha Rifles (the Sirmoor Rifles)

1936 2nd King Edward VII's Own Goorkhas (the Sirmoor Rifles)
1947 to British Army

3rd Queen Alexandra's Own Gurkha Rifles

1815 Kumaon Battalion
1816 Kumaon Provincial Battalion
1823 9th (or Kumaon) Local Battalion
1826 7th (or Kumaon) Local Battalion
1860 Kumaon Battalion
1861 18th Regiment of Bengal Native Infantry
1861 3rd Goorkha Regiment
1864 3rd (the Kumaon) Goorkha Regiment
1887 3rd Goorkha Regiment
1891 3rd Goorkha (Rifle) Regiment
1901 3rd Gurkha Rifles
1907 3rd The Queen's Own Gurkha Rifles
1908 3rd Queen Alexandra's Own Gurkha Rifles
1947 to Indian Army

4th Prince of Wales's Own Gurkha Rifles

1857 Extra Goorkha Regiment
1861 19th Regiment of Bengal Native Infantry
1861 4th Goorkha Regiment
1891 4th Gurkha (Rifle) Regiment
1901 4th Gurkha Rifles
1924 4th Prince of Wales's Own Gurkha Rifles
1947 to Indian Army

5th Royal Gurkha Rifles (Frontier Force)

1858 25th Punjab Infantry, or Hazara Goorkha Battalion
1861 7th Regiment of Infantry (or Hazara Goorkha Battalion), Punjab Irregular Force
1861 5th Goorkha Regiment, or Hazara Goorkha Battalion
1886 5th Goorkha Regiment, The Hazara Goorkha Battalion
1887 5th Goorkha Regiment
1891 5th Gurkha (Rifle) Regiment
1901 5th Gurkha Rifles
1903 5th Gurkha Rifles (Frontier Force)
1923 5th Royal Gurkha Rifles (Frontier Force)
1947 to Indian Army

6th Queen Elizabeth's Own Gurkha Rifles

1817 Cuttack Legion
1823 Rangpur Light Infantry Battalion
1826 8th (or Rangpur) Local Light Infantry Battalion
1828 8th (or Assam) Local Light Infantry Battalion
1844 1st Assam Light Infantry
1861 46th Regiment of Bengal Native Infantry
1861 42nd Regiment of Bengal Native Infantry
1864 42nd (Assam) Regiment of Bengal Native (Light) Infantry
1885 42nd (Assam) Regiment of Bengal (Light) Infantry
1886 42nd Regiment Goorkha Light Infantry
1889 42nd (Goorkha) Regiment of Bengal (Light) Infantry
1891 42nd Gurkha (Rifle) Regiment of Bengal Infantry
1901 42nd Gurkha Rifles
1903 6th Gurkha Rifles
1947 to British Army
1959 6th Queen Elizabeth's Own Gurkha Rifles

7th Duke of Edinburgh's Own Gurkha Rifles

1902 8th Gurkha Rifles
1903 2nd Battalion, 10th Gurkha Rifles
1907 7th Gurkha Rifles
1947 to British Army
1 Jan. 1959 7th Duke of Edinburgh's Own Gurkha Rifles

8th Gurkha Rifles

1st Battalion
1824 16th or Sylhet Local Battalion
1826 11th or Sylhet Local (Light) Infantry Battalion
1861 48th Regiment of Bengal Native Infantry
1861 44th Regiment of Bengal Native Infantry
1864 44th (Sylhet) Regiment of Bengal Native (Light) Infantry
1885 44th (Sylhet) Regiment of Bengal (Light) Infantry
1886 44th Regiment, Goorkha (Light) Infantry
1889 44th (Goorkha) Regiment of Bengal (Light) Infantry
1891 44th Gurkha (Rifle) Regiment of Bengal Infantry
1901 44th Gurkha Rifles
1903 8th Gurkha Rifles

1907 became the 1st Battalion, 8th Gurkha Rifles when the 2nd Battalion was raised at Gauhati

2nd Battalion
1835 Assam Sebundy Corps
1839 Lower Assam Sebundy Corps
1839 1st Assam Sebundy Corps
1844 2nd Assam Light Infantry
1861 47th Regiment of Bengal Native Infantry
1861 43rd Regiment of Bengal Native Infantry
1884 43rd (Assam) Regiment of Bengal Native (Light) Infantry
1865 43rd (Assam) Regiment of Bengal (Light) Infantry
1886 43rd Regiment Goorkha Light Infantry
1889 43rd (Goorkha) Regiment of Bengal (Light) Infantry
1891 43rd Gurkha (Rifle) Regiment of Bengal Infantry
1901 43rd Gurkha Rifles
1903 7th Gurkha Rifles
1907 became the 2nd Battalion, 8th Gurkha Rifles
1947 to Indian Army

9th Gurkha Rifles

1817 Fatehgarh Levy
1819 Manipuri Levy
1823 1st Battalion, 32nd Regiment of Bengal Native Infantry
1824 63rd Regiment of Bengal Native Infantry
1861 9th Regiment of Bengal Native Infantry
1885 9th Regiment of Bengal Infantry
1894 9th (Gurkha Rifles) Regiment of Bengal Infantry
1901 9th Gurkha Rifles
1947 to Indian Army

10th Princess Mary's Own Gurkha Rifles

1890 1st Regiment of Burma Infantry
1891 10th Regiment (1st Burma Battalion) of Madras Infantry
1892 10th Regiment (1st Burma Rifles) Madras Infantry
1895 10th Regiment (1st Burma Gurkha Rifles) Madras Infantry
1901 10th Gurkha Rifles
1947 to British Army
1949 10th Princess Mary's Own Gurkha Rifles

INDEX

References to illustrations are in *italic*.

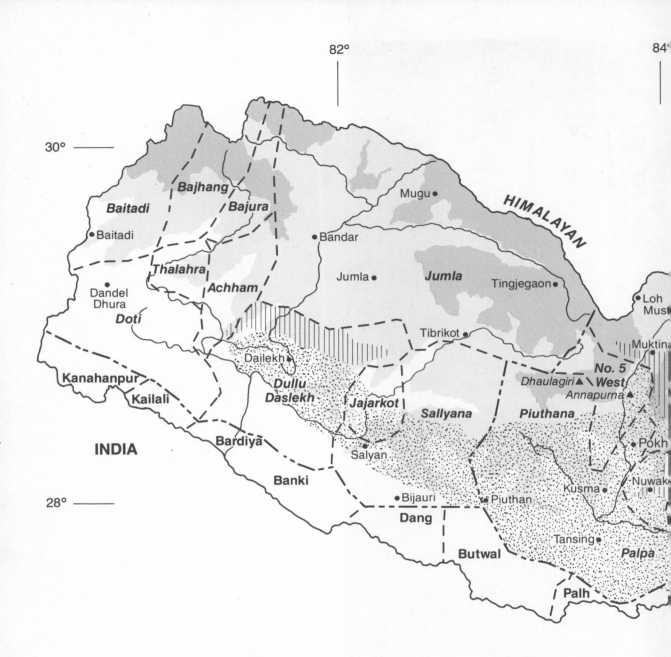
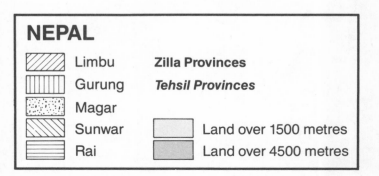